CONTENTS

CHILLI CHICKEN WRAPS

Prep: 10 mins - Cook: 25 mins - Serves 4

INGREDIENTS

- 2 tbsp vegetable oil
- 6 boneless, skinless chicken thighs, cut into bite-sized pieces
- 1 large onion, thinly sliced into half-moons
- 2 garlic cloves, finely chopped
- 3cm piece ginger, peeled and finely chopped
- ½ tsp ground cumin
- ½ tsp garam masala
- 1 tbsp tomato purée
- 1 red chilli, thinly sliced into rings
- juice ½ lemon
- 4 rotis, warmed
- ½ small red onion, chopped
- 4 tbsp mango chutney or lime pickle
- 4 handfuls mint or coriander
- 4 tbsp yogurt

DIRECTIONS

STEP 1

Heat the oil in a large frying pan over a medium heat. Add the chicken, brown on all sides, then remove. Add the onion, garlic, ginger and a pinch of salt. Cook for 5 mins or until softened.

STEP 2

Increase the heat to high. Return the chicken to the pan with the spices, tomato purée, chilli and lemon juice. Season well and cook for 10 mins or until the chicken is tender.

STEP 3

Divide the chicken, red onion, chutney, herbs and yogurt between the four warm rotis. Roll up and serve with plenty of napkins

SQUASH & SPINACH FUSILLI WITH PECANS

Prep: 10 mins - Cook: 40 mins - Serves 2

INGREDIENTS

- 160g butternut squash , diced
- 3 garlic cloves , sliced
- 1 tbsp chopped sage leaves
- 2 tsp rapeseed oil
- 1 large courgette , halved and sliced
- 6 pecan halves
- 115g wholemeal fusilli
- 125g bag baby spinach

DIRECTIONS

STEP 1

Heat oven to 200C/180C fan/gas 6. Toss the butternut squash, garlic and sage in the oil, then spread out in a roasting tin and cook in the oven for 20 mins, add the courgettes and cook for a further 15 mins. Give everything a stir, then add the pecans and cook for 5 mins more until the nuts are toasted and the vegetables are tender and starting to caramelise.

STEP 2

Meanwhile, boil the pasta according to pack instructions – about 12 mins. Drain, then tip into a serving bowl and toss with the spinach so that it wilts in the heat from the pasta. Add the roasted veg and pecans, breaking up the nuts a little, and toss again really well before serving.

ASPARAGUS & LEMON SPAGHETTI WITH PEAS

Prep: 7 mins - Cook: 12 mins - Serves 2

INGREDIENTS

- 150g wholemeal spaghetti
- 160g asparagus, ends trimmed and cut into lengths
- 2 tbsp rapeseed oil
- 2 leeks (220g), cut into lengths, then thin strips
- 1 red chilli, deseeded and finely chopped
- 1 garlic clove, finely grated
- 160g frozen peas
- 1 lemon, zested and juiced, plus wedges to serve

DIRECTIONS

STEP 1

Boil the spaghetti for 12 mins until al dente, adding the asparagus for the last 3 mins. Meanwhile, heat the oil in a large non-stick frying pan, add the leeks and chilli and cook for 5 mins. Stir in the garlic, peas and lemon zest and juice and cook for a few mins more.

STEP 2

Drain and add the pasta to the pan with ¼ mug of the pasta water and toss everything together until well mixed. Spoon into shallow bowls and serve with lemon wedges for squeezing over, if you like.

LOW-FAT MOUSSAKA

Prep: 15 mins - Cook: 40 mins - Serves 4

INGREDIENTS

- 200g frozen sliced peppers
- 3 garlic cloves , crushed
- 200g extra-lean minced beef
- 100g red lentils
- 2 tsp dried oregano , plus extra for sprinkling
- 500ml carton passata
- 1 aubergine , sliced into 1.5cm rounds
- 4 tomatoes , sliced into 1cm rounds
- 2 tsp olive oil
- 25g parmesan , finely grated
- 170g pot 0% fat Greek yogurt
- freshly grated nutmeg

DIRECTIONS

STEP 1

Cook the peppers gently in a large non-stick pan for about 5 mins – the water from them should stop them sticking. Add the garlic and cook for 1 min more, then add the beef, breaking up with a fork, and cook until brown. Tip in the lentils, half the oregano, the passata and a splash of water. Simmer for 15-20 mins until the lentils are tender, adding more water if you need to.

STEP 2

Meanwhile, heat the grill to Medium. Arrange the aubergine and tomato slices on a non-stick baking tray and brush with the oil. Sprinkle with the remaining oregano and some seasoning, then grill for 1-2 mins each side until lightly charred – you may need to do this in batches.

STEP 3

Mix half the Parmesan with the yogurt and some seasoning. Divide the beef mixture between 4 small ovenproof dishes and top with the sliced aubergine and tomato. Spoon over the yogurt topping and sprinkle with the extra oregano, Parmesan and nutmeg. Grill for 3-4 mins until bubbling. Serve with a salad, if you like.

COURGETTE, LEEK & GOAT'S CHEESE SOUP

Prep: 8 mins - Cook: 17 mins - Serves 4

INGREDIENTS

- 1 tbsp rapeseed oil
- 400g leeks, well washed and sliced
- 450g courgettes, sliced
- 3 tsp vegetable bouillon powder, made up to 1 litre with boiling water
- 400g spinach
- 150g tub soft vegetarian goat's cheese
- 15g basil, plus a few leaves to serve
- 8 tsp omega seed mix (see tip)
- 4 x 25g portions wholegrain rye bread

DIRECTIONS

STEP 1

Heat the oil in a large pan and fry the leeks for a few mins to soften. Add the courgettes, then cover the pan and cook for 5 mins more. Pour in the stock, cover and cook for about 7 mins.

STEP 2

Add the spinach, then cover the pan and cook for 5 mins so that it wilts. Take off the heat and blitz until really smooth with a hand blender. Add the goat's cheese and basil, then blitz again.

STEP 3

If you're making this recipe as part of our two-person Summer Healthy Diet Plan, spoon half the soup into two bowls or large flasks, then cool and chill the remainder for another day. Reheat in a pan or microwave to serve. If serving in bowls, scatter with some extra basil leaves and the seeds, and eat with the rye bread.

SALMON SALAD WITH SESAME DRESSING

Prep: 7 mins - Cook: 16 mins - Serves 2

INGREDIENTS

For the salad

- 250g new potatoes , sliced
- 160g French beans , trimmed
- 2 wild salmon fillets
- 80g salad leaves
- 4 small clementines , 3 sliced, 1 juiced
- handful of basil , chopped
- handful of coriander , chopped

For the dressing

- 2 tsp sesame oil
- 2 tsp tamari
- ½ lemon , juiced
- 1 red chilli , deseeded and chopped
- 2 tbsp finely chopped onion (1/4 small onion)

DIRECTIONS

STEP 1

Steam the potatoes and beans in a steamer basket set over a pan of boiling water for 8 mins. Arrange the salmon fillets on top and steam for a further 6-8 mins, or until the salmon flakes easily when tested with a fork.

STEP 2

Meanwhile, mix the dressing ingredients together along with the clementine juice. If eating straightaway, divide the salad leaves between two plates and top with the warm potatoes and beans and the clementine slices. Arrange the salmon fillets on top, scatter over the herbs and spoon over the dressing. If taking to work, prepare the potatoes, beans and salmon the night before, then pack into a rigid airtight container with the salad leaves kept separate. Put the salad elements together and dress just before eating to prevent the leaves from wilting.

THAI PRAWN & GINGER NOODLES

Prep: 15 mins - Cook: 15 mins plus soaking - Serves 2

INGREDIENTS

- 100g folded rice noodles (sen lek)
- zest and juice 1 small orange
- 1½-2 tbsp red curry paste
- 1-2 tsp fish sauce
- 2 tsp light brown soft sugar
- 1 tbsp sunflower oil
- 25g ginger, scraped and shredded
- 2 large garlic cloves, sliced
- 1 red pepper, deseeded and sliced
- 85g sugar snap peas, halved lengthways
- 140g beansprouts
- 175g pack raw king prawns
- handful chopped basil
- handful chopped coriander

DIRECTIONS

STEP 1

Put the noodles in a bowl and pour over boiling water to cover them. Set aside to soak for 10 mins. Stir together the orange juice and zest, curry paste, fish sauce, sugar and 3 tbsp water to make a sauce.

STEP 2

Heat the oil in a large wok and add half the ginger and the garlic. Cook, stirring, for 1 min. Add the pepper and stir-fry for 3 mins more. Toss in the sugar snaps, cook briefly, then pour in the curry sauce. Add the beansprouts and prawns, and continue cooking until the prawns just turn pink. Drain the noodles, then toss these into the pan with the herbs and remaining ginger. Mix until the noodles are well coated in the sauce, then serve.

EASY SOUP MAKER LENTIL SOUP

Prep: 5 mins - Cook: 30 mins - Serves 4

INGREDIENTS

- 750ml vegetable or ham stock
- 75g red lentils
- 3 carrots , finely chopped
- 1 medium leek , sliced (150g)
- small handful chopped parsley , to serve

DIRECTIONS

STEP 1

Put the stock, lentils, carrots and leek into a soup maker, and press the 'chunky soup' function. Make sure you don't fill it above the max fill line. The soup will look a little foamy to start, but don't worry – it will disappear once cooked.

STEP 2

Once the cycle is complete, check the lentils are tender, and season well. Scatter over the parsley to serve.

COD WITH CUCUMBER, AVOCADO & MANGO SALSA SALAD

Prep: 5 mins - Cook: 8 mins - Serves 2

INGREDIENTS

- 2 x skinless cod fillets
- 1 lime , zested and juiced
- 1 small mango , peeled, stoned and chopped (or 2 peaches, stoned and chopped)
- 1 small avocado , stoned, peeled and sliced

- ¼ cucumber , chopped
- 160g cherry tomatoes , quartered
- 1 red chilli , deseeded and chopped
- 2 spring onions , sliced
- handful chopped coriander

DIRECTIONS

STEP 1

Heat oven to 200C/180C fan/gas 6. Put the fish in a shallow ovenproof dish and pour over half the lime juice, with a little of the zest, then grind over some black pepper. Bake for 8 mins or until the fish flakes easily but is still moist.

STEP 2

Meanwhile, put the rest of the INGREDIENTS, plus the remaining lime juice and zest, in a bowl and combine well. Spoon onto plates and top with the cod, spooning over any juices in the dish.

SLOW COOKER MUSHROOM RISOTTO

Prep: 30 mins **Cook:** 1 hr

Serves 4

INGREDIENTS

- 1 onion, finely chopped
- 1 tsp olive oil
- 250g chestnut mushrooms, sliced
- 1l vegetable stock
- 50g porcini
- 300g wholegrain rice
- small bunch parsley, finely chopped
- grated vegetarian parmesan-style cheese to serve

DIRECTIONS

STEP 1

Heat the slow cooker if necessary. Fry the onion in the oil in a frying pan with a splash of water for 10 minutes or until it is soft but not coloured. Add the mushroom slices and stir them around until they start to soften and release their juices.

STEP 2

Meanwhile pour the stock into a saucepan and add the porcini, bring to a simmer and then leave to soak. Tip the onions and mushrooms into the slow cooker and add the rice, stir it in well. Pour over the stock and porcini leaving any bits of sediment in the saucepan (or pour the mixture through a fine sieve).

STEP 3

Cook on High for 3 hours, stirring halfway. and then check the consistency – the rice should be cooked. If it needs a little more liquid stir in a splash of stock. Stir in the parsley and season. Serve with the parmesan.

HOME-STYLE PORK CURRY WITH CAULIFLOWER RICE

Prep: 15 mins - Cook: 1 hr - Serves 4

INGREDIENTS

For the curry

- 425g lean pork fillet (tenderloin), cubed
- 2 tbsp Madras curry powder
- 2 tbsp red wine vinegar
- 1 tbsp rapeseed oil
- 1 large onion , finely chopped
- 2 tbsp finely shredded ginger
- 1 tsp fennel , toasted in a pan then crushed
- 1 tsp cumin , toasted in a pan then crushed
- 400g can chopped tomatoes
- 2 tbsp red lentils
- 350g pack baby aubergine , quartered
- 1 reduced-salt vegetable stock cube

For the cauliflower rice

- 1 medium cauliflower
- good handful coriander , chopped
- cumin seeds , toasted (optional)

DIRECTIONS

STEP 1

Tip the pork into a bowl and stir in the curry powder and vinegar. Set aside. Heat the oil in a heavy-based pan and fry the onion and ginger for 10 mins, stirring frequently, until golden. Tip in the pork mixture and fry for a few mins more. Remove the pork and set aside. Stir in the toasted spices, then tip in the tomatoes, lentils and aubergine, and crumble in the stock cube. Cover and leave to simmer for 40 mins, stirring frequently, until the aubergine is almost cooked. If it starts to look dry, add a splash of water. Return the pork to the pan and cook for a further 10-20 mins until the pork is cooked and tender.

STEP 2

Just before serving, cut the hard core and stalks from the cauliflower and pulse the rest in a food processor to make grains the size of rice. Tip into a heatproof bowl, cover with cling film, then pierce and microwave for 7 mins on High – there is no need to add any water. Stir in the coriander and serve with the curry. For spicier rice, add some toasted cumin seeds.

HAKE & SEAFOOD CATAPLANA

Prep: 15 mins - Cook: 35 mins - Serves 2

INGREDIENTS

- 2 tbsp cold-pressed rapeseed oil
- 1 onion , halved and thinly sliced
- 250g salad potatoes , cut into chunks
- 1 large red pepper , deseeded and chopped
- 1 courgette (200g), thickly sliced
- 2 tomatoes , chopped (150g)
- 2 large garlic cloves , finely grated
- 1 tbsp cider vinegar (optional)
- 2 tsp vegetable bouillon powder
- 2 skinless hake fillets (pack size 240g)
- 150g pack ready-cooked mussels (not in shells)
- 60g peeled prawns
- large handful of parsley , chopped

DIRECTIONS

STEP 1

Heat the oil in a wide non-stick pan with a tight-fitting lid. Fry the onions and potatoes for about 5 mins, or until starting to soften. Add the peppers, courgettes, tomatoes and garlic, then stir in the vinegar, if using, the bouillon and 200ml water. Bring to a simmer, cover and cook for 25 mins, or until the peppers and courgettes are very tender (if your pan doesn't have a tight-fitting lid, wet a sheet of baking parchment and place over the stew before covering – this helps keep in the juices).

STEP 2

Add the hake fillets, mussels and prawns, then cover and cook for 5 mins more, or until the fish flakes easily when tested with a fork. Scatter over the parsley and serve.

HERB & GARLIC PORK WITH SUMMER RATATOUILLE

Prep: 15 mins - Cook: 25 mins - 4 (or 2 with leftovers for other meals)

INGREDIENTS

- 2 tsp rapeseed oil
- 2 red onions , halved and sliced
- 2 peppers (any colour), diced
- 1 large aubergine , diced
- 2 large courgettes , halved and sliced
- 2 garlic cloves , chopped
- 400g can chopped tomatoes
- 2 tsp vegetable bouillon
- 1 thyme spig
- handful basil , stalks chopped, leaves torn and kept separate

For the pork

- 475g pork tenderloin, fat trimmed off, cut into 2 equal pieces
- 2 garlic cloves , crushed
- 1 tbsp thyme leaves , plus a few sprigs to decorate
- 1 tsp rapeseed oil
- brown rice or new potatoes, to serve

DIRECTIONS

STEP 1

Heat the oil in a large non-stick pan and fry the onions for 5 mins or until softened. Stir in the peppers, aubergine, courgettes and garlic, and cook, stirring, for a few mins. Tip in the tomatoes and 1 can of water, then stir in the bouillon, thyme and basil stalks. Cover and simmer for 20 mins or until tender. Stir through the basil leaves.

STEP 2

Meanwhile, rub the pork with the garlic, then scatter with the thyme and some black pepper, patting it so it sticks all over. Heat the oil in a non-stick frying pan and cook the pork for about 12 mins, turning frequently so it browns on all sides, until tender but still moist. Cover and rest for 5 mins.

STEP 3

If you're making this as part of the Healthy Diet Plan, set aside half of the pork to use in the curried pork bulghar salad later in the week and store in the fridge once cooled. Chill the half of the ratatouille and use it to make the ratatouille pasta salad with rocket for another day. If you are serving four you can skip this step.

STEP 4

To serve, slice the pork and serve with the ratatouille, some brown rice or new potatoes and some extra thyme.

SMASHED CHICKEN WITH CORN SLAW

Prep: 10 mins - Cook: 5 mins - Serves 4

INGREDIENTS

For the chicken

- 4 skinless chicken breast fillets
- 1 lime , zested and juiced
- 2 tbsp bio yogurt
- 1 tsp fresh thyme leaves
- ¼ tsp turmeric
- 2 tbsp finely chopped coriander
- 1 garlic clove , finely grated
- 1 tsp rapeseed oil

For the slaw

- 1 small avocado
- 1 lime , zested and juiced
- 2 tbsp bio yogurt
- 2 tbsp finely chopped coriander
- 160g corn , cut from 2 cobs
- 1 red pepper , deseeded and chopped

- 1 red onion , halved and finely sliced
- 320g white cabbage , finely sliced
- 150g new potatoes , boiled, to serve

DIRECTIONS

STEP 1

Cut the chicken breasts in half, then put them between two sheets of baking parchment and bash with a rolling pin to flatten. Mix the lime zest and juice with the yogurt, thyme, turmeric, coriander and garlic in a large bowl. Add the chicken and stir until well coated. Leave to marinate while you make the slaw.

STEP 2

Mash the avocado with the lime juice and zest, 2 tbsp yogurt and the coriander. Stir in the corn, red pepper, onion and cabbage.

STEP 3

Heat a large non-stick frying pan or griddle pan, then cook the chicken in batches for a few mins each side – they'll cook quickly as they're thin. Serve the hot chicken with the slaw and the new potatoes. If you're cooking for two, chill half the chicken and slaw for lunch another day (eat within two days).

SPICY CHICKEN & BEAN STEW

Prep: 15 mins - Cook: 1 hr and 20 mins - Serves 6

INGREDIENTS

- 1¼ kg chicken thighs and drumsticks (approx. weight, we used a 1.23kg mixed pack)
- 1 tbsp olive oil
- 2 onions, sliced
- 1 garlic clove, crushed
- 2 red chillies, deseeded and chopped
- 250g frozen peppers, defrosted
- 400g can chopped tomatoes
- 420g can kidney beans in chilli sauce
- 2 x 400g cans butter beans, drained
- 400ml hot chicken stock
- small bunch coriander, chopped
- 150ml pot soured cream and crusty bread, to serve

DIRECTIONS

STEP 1

Pull the skin off the chicken and discard. Heat the oil in a large casserole dish, brown the chicken all over, then remove with a slotted spoon. Tip in the onions, garlic and chillies, then fry for 5 mins until starting to soften and turn golden.

STEP 2

Add the peppers, tomatoes, beans and hot stock. Put the chicken back on top, half-cover with a pan lid and cook for 50 mins, until the chicken is cooked through and tender.

STEP 3

Stir through the coriander and serve with soured cream and crusty bread.

ORANGE & RASPBERRY GRANOLA

Prep: 15 mins - Cook: 25 mins plus at least 1 hr chilling - Serves 4

INGREDIENTS

- 400g jumbo oats
- juice 2 oranges (150ml), plus zest of 1/2
- 1 tsp ground cinnamon
- 2 tbsp freeze-dried raspberries or strawberries (see tip)
- 25g flaked almonds , toasted
- 25g mixed seeds (such as sunflower, pumpkin, sesame and linseed)

To serve

- 2 large oranges , peeled and segmented
- mint leaves (optional)

DIRECTIONS

STEP 1

Put 200g oats and 500ml water in a food processor and blitz for 1 min. Line a sieve with clean muslin and pour in the oat mixture. Leave to drip through for 5 mins, then twist the ends of the muslin and squeeze well to capture as much of the oat milk as possible – it should be the consistency of single cream. Best chilled at least 1 hr before serving. Can be kept in a sealed or covered jug in the fridge for up to 3 days.

STEP 2

Heat oven to 200C/180C fan/gas 6 and line a baking tray with baking parchment. Put the orange juice in a medium saucepan and bring to the boil. Boil rapidly for 5 mins or until the liquid has reduced by half, stirring occasionally. Mix the remaining 200g oats with the orange zest and cinnamon. Remove the pan from the heat and stir the oat mixture into the juice. Spread over the lined tray in a thin layer and bake for 10-15 mins or until lightly browned and crisp, turning the oats every few mins. Leave to cool on the tray.

STEP 3

Once cool, mix the oats with the raspberries, flaked almonds and seeds. Can be kept in a sealed jar for up to one week. To serve, spoon the granola into bowls, pour over the oat milk and top with the orange segments and mint leaves, if you like.

HERBY CHICKEN GYROS

Prep: 10 mins - Cook: 4 mins - Serves 2

INGREDIENTS

- 1 large skinless chicken breast
- rapeseed oil , for brushing
- small garlic clove , crushed
- ½ tsp dried oregano
- 2 tbsp Greek yogurt
- 10 cm piece cucumber , grated, excess juice squeezed out
- 2 tbsp chopped mint , plus a few leaves to serve
- 2 wholemeal pitta breads
- 2 red or yellow tomatoes , sliced
- 1 red pepper from a jar (not in oil), deseeded and sliced

DIRECTIONS

STEP 1

Cut the chicken breast in half lengthways, then cover with cling film and bash with a rolling pin to flatten it. Brush with some oil, then cover with the garlic, oregano and some pepper. Heat a non-stick frying pan and cook the chicken for a few mins each side. Meanwhile, mix the yogurt, cucumber and mint to make tzatziki.

STEP 2

Cut the tops from the pittas along their longest side and stuff with the chicken, tomato, pepper and tzatziki. Poke in a few mint leaves to serve. If taking to the office for lunch, pack the tzatziki in a separate pot and add just before eating to prevent the pitta going soggy before lunchtime.

RYE PIZZA WITH FIGS, FENNEL, GORGONZOLA & HAZELNUTS

Prep: 1 hr - Cook: 45 mins plus 2-3 hrs rising - makes 2 x 30cm pizzas

INGREDIENTS

For the dough

- 5g active dried yeast
- 250g strong white flour
- 125g '00' flour
- 125g rye flour
- ½ tsp sugar
- 1 tsp olive oil
- semolina flour , for dusting

For the topping

- 1 large fennel bulb , any fronds reserved
- juice 1/2 small lemon
- 1 tbsp olive oil
- 2 medium onions , halved and very finely sliced
- ¼ tsp fennel seeds , coarsely crushed in a mortar
- a little extra virgin olive oil , for drizzling
- 12 small figs , halved
- 1 ½ tbsp balsamic vinegar
- a little caster sugar , for sprinkling
- 180g gorgonzola (or vegetarian alternative), broken into chunks
- 2 tbsp hazelnuts , halved and toasted

DIRECTIONS

STEP 1

To make the dough, mix the yeast in a small bowl with 2 tbsp warm water and 1 tbsp strong white flour. Leave somewhere warm to 'sponge' for 20 mins or so (this dissolves and activates the yeast). Tip the three flours into a large bowl and make a well in the centre. Pour in the sponged yeast, 1 tsp salt, sugar, oil and 290ml warm water, and mix to form a wet dough. Knead for 10 mins until satiny and elastic, then put in a clean bowl, cover with a cloth and leave to double in size for 2 1/2 - 3 hrs.

STEP 2

Quarter the fennel bulb lengthways and remove any tough outer leaves. Trim the base of each, thinly slice with a knife or mandolin, then put in a bowl with the lemon juice so it doesn't turn brown.

STEP 3

Heat the oil in a frying pan, add the onions and a pinch of salt, and fry over a medium heat for 7 mins. Add 1-2 tbsp of water, season with pepper, cover and cook on a low heat for 10 mins until softened. Add most of the fennel, along with the fennel seeds and seasoning, and cook for 3 mins, stirring every so often. If the mixture is still wet, uncover and bubble off any liquid.

STEP 4

An hour before cooking, heat the oven to its highest setting and put a baking sheet or pizza stone in to heat. Tip the dough onto a lightly floured surface, knead it a little, then halve and roll each piece into a circle or rough square. Lift the dough and, while rotating, stretch with your fingertips until each piece is 30-32cm across and as thin as possible with a slightly thicker edge.

STEP 5

Sprinkle two large baking sheets with semolina and put the pizza bases on them. Top each base with the cooked onion and fennel mix, then the pieces of raw fennel, leaving a 3cm border. Drizzle with a little olive oil. Put the halved figs on top and spoon on a little balsamic vinegar and a sprinkle of sugar. Grind over some pepper. Carefully slide the first pizza onto the heated baking sheet in the oven. Bake for 8-12 mins until the dough is golden and the figs caramelised. Halfway through the cooking time, dot the pizza with the cheese. Scatter on the toasted hazelnuts and any reserved fennel fronds. Repeat with the second pizza.

BACON & MUSHROOM RISOTTO

Prep: 10 mins - Cook: 30 mins - Serves 4

INGREDIENTS

- 1 tbsp olive oil
- 1 onion, chopped
- 8 rashers streaky bacon, chopped
- 250g chestnut mushroom, sliced
- 300g risotto rice
- 1l hot chicken stock
- grated parmesan, to serve

DIRECTIONS

STEP 1

Heat the oil in a deep frying pan and cook the onion and bacon for 5 mins to soften. Add the mushrooms and cook for a further 5 mins until they start to release their juices. Stir in the rice and cook until all the juices have been absorbed.

STEP 2

Add the stock, a ladleful at a time, stirring well and waiting for most of the stock to be absorbed before adding the next ladleful – it will take about 20 mins for all the stock to be added. Once the rice is cooked, season and serve with the grated Parmesan.

STUFFED PORCHETTA

Prep: 30 mins - Cook: 3 hrs and 5 mins plus at least 8 hrs chilling, 1 hr standing and 30 mins resting - Serves 6 - 8

INGREDIENTS

- 1 ½kg bone-out pork belly
- 1 tbsp bicarbonate of soda
- 3 tsp fennel seeds
- 1 tsp chilli flakes

For the stuffing

- 1 tbsp extra virgin olive oil
- 1 medium onion , finely chopped
- ½ fennel bulb , hard core cut out and discarded, the rest finely chopped
- ½ tsp coriander seeds , crushed
- 2 garlic cloves , crushed
- 250g minced pork shoulder
- 1 slice sourdough bread, torn into small pieces
- 25g toasted pine nuts
- grated zest 1 unwaxed orange
- 3 dried apricots , finely chopped
- 3 sage leaves , finely chopped
- ½ tbsp rosemary leaves, chopped
- ½ tbsp lemon juice
- freshly grated nutmeg
- 1 egg , beaten

DIRECTIONS

STEP 1

Score the pork belly skin with a sharp knife in a cross pattern. Score down to just before where the skin meets the fat, rather than the fat itself. Bring a large saucepan of water to a simmer and add the bicarbonate of soda. Lower the pork into the water, poach gently for 5 mins, then remove it from the water and leave to cool to room temperature.

STEP 2

Meanwhile, toast the fennel seeds and chilli flakes in a dry frying pan over a high heat for 1-2 mins, then tip into a bowl and leave to cool. Grind the spices in a spice grinder or with a pestle and mortar, then mix with 1 tbsp fine sea salt.

STEP 3

Once the pork has cooled, turn it skin-side down and pierce the underside of the meat all over with a knife. Rub the meat with the spiced salt rub, cover and put it in the fridge for at least 8 hrs or overnight. Can be prepared 24 hours ahead.

STEP 4

The next day, make your stuffing. Heat the olive oil in a non-stick frying pan and add the onion and fennel. Season and cook gently over a low heat for 10 mins. Add the coriander seeds and garlic, and cook for another 2 mins, then add the mince. Cook for 8-10 mins until the mince is browned. Set aside and leave to cool.

STEP 5

Transfer the mince and onion mix to a bowl and add the sourdough, pine nuts, orange zest, apricots, herbs, lemon juice and nutmeg. Season well, then mix together thoroughly with your hands. Add the egg and mix again.

STEP 6

Lie the pork belly on a board, skin-side down. Form the stuffing into a sausage shape running all the way down the middle of the belly. Wrap the sides of the belly around the stuffing and tie with butcher's string. Place seam-side down in a roasting tin, uncovered, and chill for at least 2 hrs, preferably overnight. You want the skin to dry out completely so that it crisps up when you roast it.

STEP 7

To cook the pork, remove it from the fridge and leave it for at least 1 hr to come to room temperature before you cook it. Heat oven to 180C/160C fan/ gas 4 and cook the pork for about 2 hrs, turning the tin every 30 mins or so. After 2 hrs, turn the heat up to 220C/ 200C fan/gas 7 and cook for another 20 mins. When the pork is done, a thermometer pushed into its centre should read 77C. If the skin looks in danger of burning, cover it with foil – but only do this once it has crackled.

STEP 8

Once the pork has cooked, remove from the oven and leave to rest for 30 mins. When you're ready to carve, put the pork on a big chopping board. Using a sharp knife, slice the meat into rounds.

SEA BREAM IN CRAZY WATER (ORATA ALL'ACQUA PAZZA)

Prep: 10 mins - Cook: 30 mins - Serves 4

INGREDIENTS

- 4 tbsp good quality extra-virgin olive oil
- 2 whole sea bream or sea bass (about 450g each), gutted and cleaned
- 2 garlic cloves , finely sliced
- ½ small red chilli , chopped
- 400g small tomato (a mix of different-coloured cherry tomatoes would be best)
- 4 tbsp white wine
- small handful capers
- chopped parsley

DIRECTIONS

STEP 1

Heat half the oil in a large, lidded frying pan. Carefully slip the fish into the sizzling oil and cook for 4-5 mins until starting to brown. Flip over and scatter the garlic around the fish. Sizzle for 1 min more, then add the chilli and scatter over the tomatoes. Pour over the wine and let it bubble for 1 min, then pour over 100ml water and season generously with sea salt and pepper.

STEP 2

Put on the lid, turn up the heat and simmer for 15 mins until the fish is cooked through – you can tell when the eyes turn bright white and the flesh feels softer.

STEP 3

Lift each fish out the pan onto a serving plate and put the pan back on the heat. Add the capers and parsley, and boil hard for 1 min. You can now serve the fish and the sauce separately or slip them back into the pan, spoon some of the sauce over and bring the pan to the table. Drizzle with a little more oil just before serving.

CREAMY CHICKEN & GREEN BEAN PESTO PASTA

Prep: 10 mins - Cook: 10 mins - Serves 4

INGREDIENTS

- 400g pasta shapes
- 250g green bean, trimmed
- 1 tbsp olive oil
- 1 bunch spring onions, finely sliced
- 2 large ready-roasted chicken breasts, shredded
- 5 tbsp pesto
- 3 tbsp double cream
- handful parmesan, grated, to serve

DIRECTIONS

STEP 1

Cook pasta following pack instructions, adding green beans for the final 6 mins of cooking time. Drain and reserve a few tbsps of the cooking water.

STEP 2

Meanwhile, heat olive oil in a large frying pan. Add spring onions and cook for 1-2 mins until soft, then set aside.

STEP 3

Add the shredded chicken in the pan and heat through. Stir through pesto and cream. Pop pasta and beans in with the chicken mix and stir to coat, adding a little of the cooking water. Season and sprinkle with Parmesan.

GNOCCHI WITH COURGETTE, MASCARPONE & SPRING ONIONS

Prep: 5 mins - Cook: 15 mins - Serves 2

INGREDIENTS

- 300g fresh gnocchi
- 1 tbsp olive oil
- 1 red chilli , sliced, deseeded if you like
- 1 medium courgette , cut into thin ribbons with a peeler
- 4 spring onions , chopped
- zest 1 lemon
- 2 heaped tbsp mascarpone
- 50g parmesan (or vegetarian alternative), grated
- dressed mixed leaves , to serve

DIRECTIONS

STEP 1

Cook the gnocchi following pack instructions. Drain, reserving a ladle of the cooking water, and set aside.

STEP 2

Heat the oil in a frying pan. Cook chilli and courgette for 3 mins until soft. Add spring onions, zest, mascarpone, half the Parmesan and cooking water. Mix until smooth, add gnocchi and heat through.

STEP 3

Season, divide between 2 ovenproof dishes and scatter with the remaining Parmesan. Grill for 2-3 mins until bubbling and serve with the dressed mixed leaves.

PANCAKE CANNELLONI

Prep: 30 mins - Cook: 30 mins - Serves 4

INGREDIENTS

- 420g pack free-range pork meatballs
- 400g bag fresh spinach
- 2 tbsp basil pesto
- 250g tub ricotta
- 1 egg , beaten
- ¼ tsp ground nutmeg
- 8 pre-made pancakes

- 500g carton passata
- 1 garlic clove , crushed
- 125g ball mozzarella , torn
- 1 bunch of basil , leaves only

DIRECTIONS

STEP 1

Heat the grill to high and cook the meatballs for 12-15 mins on a baking tray or following pack instructions. Cut each one in half and set aside.

STEP 2

Tip the spinach into a large colander over the sink. Pour boiling water over to wilt it and leave to drain thoroughly. When cool enough to handle, squeeze out any excess liquid and chop finely. Mix the spinach with the pesto, ricotta, egg and nutmeg, then season to taste.

STEP 3

Heat oven to 190C/170C fan/gas 5. Pour the passata over the bottom of an ovenproof dish and stir in the garlic. Divide the spinach mixture between the pancakes, spreading it out in a long strip in the centre. Add meatball pieces to each one, then roll the pancake up to seal in the filling. Lay the stuffed pancakes on the passata base and top with the mozzarella. Bake for 30 mins until the cheese is melted and bubbling. Scatter over basil leaves to serve.

GNOCCHI WITH PANCETTA, SPINACH & PARMESAN CREAM

Total time 15 mins - Serves 4

INGREDIENTS

- 500g pack gnocchi
- 1 garlic clove, sliced
- 1 tbsp olive oil
- 100ml double cream
- freshly grated nutmeg
- 130g pack smoked pancetta cubes
- 100g spinach
- zest ½ lemon

- 25g parmesan, grated, plus extra for serving
- 25g toasted pine nut

DIRECTIONS

STEP 1

Cook the gnocchi following pack instructions, then drain. Meanwhile, heat 1 tsp of the oil in a small pan and fry the garlic, then add the cream and a good grating of nutmeg. Put to one side.

STEP 2

Heat 2 tsp of the remaining oil in a frying pan and cook the pancetta until crisp. Add the gnocchi and fry until it starts to turn golden, adding a little more oil if it begins to stick. Stir in the spinach, lemon zest and seasoning.

STEP 3

Stir the Parmesan into the cream sauce. Spoon the gnocchi onto plates, drizzle over the sauce and scatter with pine nuts. Serve with extra Parmesan.

ORANGE POLENTA CAKE

Prep: 20 mins - Cook: 45 mins - Serves 8 - 10

INGREDIENTS

- 250g unsalted butter
- 250g golden caster sugar
- 4 large eggs
- 140g polenta
- 200g plain flour
- 2 tsp baking powder
- zest and juice 2 oranges (less 100ml juice for the glaze)

For the orange glaze

- 100ml orange juice
- 100g golden caster sugar

DIRECTIONS

STEP 1

Heat oven to 160C/140C fan/gas 3. Line the base and sides of a round 23cm cake tin with baking parchment. Cream the butter and sugar together until light and fluffy. Add the eggs one at a time and mix thoroughly. Once the mixture is combined, add all the dry INGREDIENTS and the zest and juice after you have measured off 100ml for the glaze.

STEP 2

Transfer the mixture to the tin, spread evenly, then cook for about 45 mins or until a skewer inserted into the centre of the cake comes out clean. Remove from the oven and turn out onto a wire rack to cool.

STEP 3

To make the glaze, put the juice and sugar in a medium saucepan and bring to the boil. Let it simmer for 5 mins, then remove from the heat and allow to cool. Drizzle the orange glaze over the top of the cooled cake. Serve with Lemon ice cream, below.

ORECCHIETTE WITH ANCHOVIES & PURPLE SPROUTING BROCCOLI

Prep: 10 mins - Cook: 15 mins - Serves 2

INGREDIENTS

- 200g orecchiette
- 4 tbsp olive oil
- 6 anchovy fillets in oil, chopped (reserve 1 tbsp oil)
- 4 fat garlic cloves , thinly sliced
- 1 red chilli , thinly sliced
- zest 1 lemon , plus juice ½
- 50g fresh breadcrumb
- 200g purple sprouting broccoli

DIRECTIONS

STEP 1

Cook the orecchiette following pack instructions. Meanwhile, heat 3 tbsp of the olive oil and 1 tbsp of the oil from the anchovies in a frying pan. Add the garlic and chilli, and sizzle for 3-4 mins until the garlic is just starting to turn golden. Add the anchovies and lemon juice, and cook for 1-2 mins more until the anchovies melt into the sauce. Put the remaining olive oil, breadcrumbs and lemon zest in another frying pan, stir together and cook until crisp.

STEP 2

When the pasta has 4-5 mins to go, add the broccoli to the pan. When cooked, drain, reserving a cup of the pasta water, then add to the frying pan with the garlic and anchovies. Stir and cook over a low heat for a further 2 mins, adding a splash of pasta water if it looks dry. Season, then serve in pasta bowls with the lemony crumbs sprinkled over the top.

LIGHTER CHICKEN CACCIATORE

Prep: 15 mins Cook: 50 mins - Serves 4

INGREDIENTS

- 1 tbsp olive oil
- 3 slices prosciutto, fat removed, chopped
- 1 medium onion, chopped
- 2 garlic cloves, finely chopped
- 2 sage sprigs
- 2 rosemary sprigs
- 4 skinless chicken breasts (550g total weight), preferably organic
- 150ml dry white wine
- 400g can plum tomatoes in natural juice
- 1 tbsp tomato purée
- 225g chestnut mushrooms, quartered or halved if large
- small handful chopped flat-leaf parsley, to serve

DIRECTIONS

STEP 1

Heat the oil in a large non-stick frying pan. Tip in the prosciutto and fry for about 2 mins until crisp. Remove with a slotted spoon, letting any fat drain back into the pan, and set aside. Put the onion, garlic and herbs in the pan and fry for 3-4 mins.

STEP 2

Spread the onion out in the pan, then lay the chicken breasts on top. Season with pepper and fry for 5 mins over a medium heat, turning the chicken once, until starting to brown on both sides and the onion is caramelising on the bottom of the pan. Remove the chicken and set aside on a plate. Raise the heat, give it a quick stir and, when sizzling, pour in the wine and let it bubble for 2 mins to reduce slightly.

STEP 3

Lower the heat to medium, return the prosciutto to the pan, then stir in the tomatoes (breaking them up with your spoon), tomato purée and mushrooms. Spoon 4 tbsp of water into the empty tomato can, swirl it around, then pour it into the pan. Cover and simmer for 15-20 mins or until the sauce has thickened and reduced slightly, then return the chicken to the pan and cook, uncovered, for about 15 mins or until the chicken is cooked through. Season and scatter over the parsley to serve.

STRAWBERRY PANNA COTTA

Prep: 30 mins - Cook: 25 mins plus cooling and 3 hrs chilling - Serves 6

INGREDIENTS

For the panna cotta

- 3 gelatine leaves
- 450ml double cream
- 200ml whole milk
- 100g white caster sugar
- 1 vanilla pod

For the strawberries

- 400g strawberry , hulled and halved, or quartered if very large
- 1 ½ tsp cornflour
- 50g white caster sugar

DIRECTIONS

STEP 1

For the panna cotta, put the gelatine leaves in a small bowl of cold water to soften – this will take about 5 mins. Meanwhile, pour the cream, milk and sugar into a pan, split the vanilla pod, scrape out the seeds and add, along with the pod, to the cream mixture. Heat gently until hot, but not bubbling. Remove the gelatine leaves from the water, squeeze out any excess liquid then add, one at a time, to the hot cream. Stir until dissolved. Leave to stand for 20-30 mins until cooled – the vanilla pods should be suspended in the liquid by this point. Strain the mixture through a sieve into 6 serving glasses, then chill for at least 3 hrs.

STEP 2

Toss the strawberries with the cornflour and sugar in a saucepan. Place over a medium heat and cook for 4-5 mins, until the released juices thicken and the strawberries soften. Set aside to cool. Once completely cooled, top the set panna cottas with the strawberry mixture. Chill until ready to serve.

BEEFY MELANZANE PARMIGIANA

Prep: 20 mins - Cook: 1 hr and 50 mins - Serves 6

INGREDIENTS

- 2 tbsp olive oil , plus extra for brushing
- 800g beef mince
- 3 garlic cloves , crushed
- 3 thyme sprigs
- 3 rosemary sprigs
- 3 bay leaves
- 2 x 400g cans chopped tomato
- glass of red wine
- 1 beef stock cube
- 1 tbsp sugar
- 5 aubergines , sliced lengthways into 5mm slices
- 2 x 125g balls mozzarella , torn into small chunks
- 50g parmesan , grated
- 250g tub mascarpone

DIRECTIONS

STEP 1

Heat the oil in a large frying pan or flameproof casserole dish. Add the mince and brown over a high heat, breaking up with a wooden spoon as you go. (You may need to do this in batches.) Once well browned, tip onto a plate.

STEP 2

Add the remaining oil, the garlic and herbs to the pan and gently cook for 1 min. Tip in the tomatoes and red wine, and bring to a simmer, stirring up any meaty bits stuck to the bottom of the pan. Return the mince to the pan, crumble in the stock cube, and add sugar and seasoning. Gently simmer for at least 1 hr, stirring occasionally, splashing in more water to keep it saucy if you need to. If you have time to simmer for longer, go for it – the longer the better. Fish out the herb stalks and bay leaves.

STEP 3

Meanwhile, heat a griddle or frying pan. Brush the aubergine slices on both sides with olive oil, then griddle in batches. You want each slice softened and slightly charred, so don't have the heat too high or the aubergine will char before softening. Remove to a plate as you go.

STEP 4

Heat oven to 180C/160C fan/gas 4. Set aside some of each cheese to go on the top. In a large baking dish spread a spoonful of mince sauce over the base then top with a layer of aubergines and season well. Spoon over some more mince sauce, then scatter over some mozzarella, Parmesan and blobs of mascarpone. Add another layer of aubergines and some seasoning. Repeat, layering everything up and finish with a layer of meat sauce. Top with your reserved cheese and bake for 30-40 mins until the top is crisp and golden and mince bubbling.

SEARED STEAK WITH CELERY & PEPPER CAPONATA

Prep: 10 mins - Cook: 30 mins - Serves 2

INGREDIENTS

- 200g extra-lean fillet steak
- 140g fresh spinach
- For the caponata
- 1-cal oil spray
- 1 red onion , halved and sliced
- 2 garlic cloves , cut into slivers
- 400g can chopped tomato
- 2 celery sticks, sliced
- 1 orange pepper , deseeded, quartered and sliced
- 25g pitted black kalamata olive , halved (about 8)
- 1 tbsp caper
- ½ tsp dried oregano or 1 tbsp fresh
- 1 tsp balsamic vinegar

DIRECTIONS

STEP 1

For the caponata, spray a large, wide non-stick pan with 3 sprays of oil, and add the onion and garlic. Cover and cook for 5 mins, stirring halfway through to brown them.

STEP 2

Tip in the tomatoes and a can of water, then stir in all the other caponata ingredients. Cover the pan and leave to simmer for 30 mins.

STEP 3

Heat a griddle or small non-stick frying pan. Generously grind black pepper over the steak and sear on both sides, about 6 mins in total, until cooked to your liking. Allow to rest while you wilt the spinach in a covered pan on a low heat.

STEP 4

Spoon the caponata onto 2 serving plates, top with the spinach, then slice the beef and arrange on top.

SAUSAGE SANDWICH WITH PESTO

Prep: 5 mins - Cook: 10 mins - Serves 1

INGREDIENTS

- 2 herby Cumberland sausages , sliced in half lengthways
- 1 ciabatta roll , sliced in half
- 2 tbsp fresh pesto
- 1 roasted red pepper from a jar, sliced in half
- ½ x 125g ball mozzarella , sliced
- handful rocket

DIRECTIONS

STEP 1

Heat grill to high. Put the sausages on a baking sheet, cut-side down, and grill for 5-6 mins or until cooked through, then set aside. Lay the ciabatta roll halves, cut-side up, on a baking tray and spread each with pesto. Top each half with a pepper and mozzarella slice, then grill for 2 mins or until golden and bubbling. Add the sausages and a handful of rocket, and put the roll back together, pressing down firmly to hold the fillings in place.

SPICY MEATBALLS WITH CHILLI BLACK BEANS

Prep: 20 mins - Cook: 25 mins - Serves 4

INGREDIENTS

- 1 red onion, halved and sliced

- 2 garlic cloves, sliced
- 1 large yellow pepper, quartered, deseeded and diced
- 1 tsp ground cumin
- 2-3 tsp chipotle chilli paste
- 300ml reduced-salt chicken stock
- 400g can cherry tomatoes
- 400g can black beans or red kidney beans, drained
- 1 avocado, stoned, peeled and chopped
- juice ½ lime

For the meatballs

- 500g pack turkey breast mince
- 50g porridge oats
- 2 spring onions, finely chopped
- 1 tsp ground cumin
- 1 tsp coriander
- small bunch coriander, chopped, stalks and leaves kept separate
- 1 tsp rapeseed oil

DIRECTIONS

STEP 1

First make the meatballs. Tip the mince into a bowl, add the oats, spring onions, spices and the coriander stalks, then lightly knead the ingredients together until well mixed. Shape into 12 ping-pong- sized balls. Heat the oil in a non-stick frying pan, add the meatballs and cook, turning them frequently, until golden. Remove from the pan.

STEP 2

Tip the onion and garlic into the pan with the pepper and stir-fry until softened. Stir in the cumin and chilli paste, then pour in the stock. Return the meatballs to the pan and cook, covered, over a low heat for 10 mins. Stir in the tomatoes and beans, and cook, uncovered, for a few mins more. Toss the avocado chunks in the lime juice and serve the meatballs topped with the avocado and coriander leaves.

SLOW COOKER SHEPHERD'S PIE

Prep: 1 hr - Cook: 5 hrs - Serves 4

INGREDIENTS

- 1 tbsp olive oil
- 1 onion, finely chopped
- 3-4 thyme sprigs
- 2 carrots, finely diced
- 250g lean (10%) mince lamb or beef
- 1 tbsp plain flour
- 1 tbsp tomato purée
- 400g can lentils, or white beans
- 1 tsp Worcestershire sauce

For the topping

- 650g potatoes, peeled and cut into chunks
- 250g sweet potatoes, peeled and cut into chunks
- 2 tbsp half-fat crème fraîche

DIRECTIONS

STEP 1

Heat the slow cooker if necessary. Heat the oil in a large frying pan. Tip the onions and thyme sprigs and fry for 2-3 mins. Then add the carrots and fry together, stirring occasionally until the vegetables start to brown. Stir in the mince and fry for 1-2 mins until no longer pink. Stir in the flour then cook for another 1-2 mins. Stir in the tomato purée and lentils and season with pepper and the Worcestershire sauce, adding a splash of water if you think the mixture is too dry. Scrape everything into the slow cooker.

STEP 2

Meanwhile cook both lots of potatoes in simmering water for 12-13 minutes or until they are cooked through. Drain well and then mash with the crème fraîche. Spoon this on top of the mince mixture and cook on Low for 5 hours - the mixture should be bubbling at the sides when it is ready. Crisp up the potato topping under the grill if you like.

CURRIED SPINACH, EGGS & CHICKPEAS

Prep: 15 mins - Cook: 35 mins - Serves 2

INGREDIENTS

- 1 tbsp rapeseed oil
- 1 onion , thinly sliced
- 1 garlic clove , crushed

- 3cm piece ginger , peeled and grated
- 1 tsp ground turmeric
- 1 tsp ground coriander
- 1 tsp garam masala
- 1 tbsp ground cumin
- 450g tomatoes , chopped
- 400g can chickpeas , drained
- 1 tsp sugar
- 200g spinach
- 2 large eggs
- 3 tbsp natural yogurt
- 1 red chilli , finely sliced
- ½ small bunch of coriander , torn

DIRECTIONS

STEP 1

Heat the oil in a large frying pan or flameproof casserole pot over a medium heat, and fry the onion for 10 mins until golden and sticky. Add the garlic, ginger, turmeric, ground coriander, garam masala, cumin and tomatoes, and fry for 2 mins more. Add the chickpeas, 100ml water and the sugar and bring to a simmer. Stir in the spinach, then cover and cook for 20-25 mins. Season to taste.

STEP 2

Cook the eggs in a pan of boiling water for 7 mins, then rinse under cold running water to cool. Drain, peel and halve. Swirl the yogurt into the curry, then top with the eggs, chilli and coriander. Season.

CABBAGE SOUP

Prep: 20 mins - Cook: 50 mins |Serves 6

INGREDIENTS

- 2 tbsp olive oil
- 1 large onion , finely chopped
- 2 celery sticks , finely chopped
- 1 large carrot , finely chopped
- 70g smoked pancetta , diced (optional)
- 1 large Savoy cabbage , shredded
- 2 fat garlic cloves , crushed

- 1 heaped tsp sweet smoked paprika
- 1 tbsp finely chopped rosemary
- 1 x 400g can chopped tomatoes
- 1.7l hot vegetable stock
- 1 x 400g can chickpeas , drained and rinsed
- shaved parmesan (or vegetarian alternative), to serve (optional)
- crusty bread , to serve (optional)

DIRECTIONS

STEP 1

Heat the oil in a casserole pot over a low heat. Add the onion, celery and carrot, along with a generous pinch of salt, and fry gently for 15 mins, or until the veg begins to soften. If you're using pancetta, add it to the pan, turn up the heat and fry for a few mins more until turning golden brown. Tip in the cabbage and fry for 5 mins, then stir through the garlic, paprika and rosemary and cook for 1 min more.

STEP 2

Tip the chopped tomatoes and stock into the pan. Bring to a simmer, then cook, uncovered, for 30 mins, adding the chickpeas for the final 10 mins. Season generously with salt and black pepper.

STEP 3

Ladle the soup into six deep bowls. Serve with the shaved parmesan and crusty bread, if you like.

RED PEPPER, SQUASH & HARISSA SOUP

Prep: 15 mins - Cook: 1 hr - Serves 6

INGREDIENTS

- 1 small butternut squash (about 600-700g), peeled and cut into chunks
- 2 red pepper , roughly chopped
- 2 red onion , roughly chopped
- 3 tbsp rapeseed oil
- 3 garlic cloves in their skins
- 1 tbsp ground coriander
- 2 tsp ground cumin
- 1.2l chicken or vegetable stock
- 2 tbsp harissa paste
- 50ml double cream

DIRECTIONS

STEP 1

Heat oven to 180C/160C fan/gas 4. Put all the veg on a large baking tray and toss together with rapeseed oil, garlic cloves in their skins, ground coriander, ground cumin and some seasoning. Roast for 45 mins, moving the veg around in the tray after 30 mins, until soft and starting to caramelise. Squeeze the garlic cloves out of their skins. Tip everything into a large pan. Add the chicken or vegetable stock, harissa paste and double cream. Bring to a simmer and bubble for a few mins. Blitz the soup in a blender, check the seasoning and add more liquid if you need to. Serve swirled with extra cream and harissa.

WARM CHERRY & BROWN SUGAR COMPOTE

Prep: 5 mins - Cook: 15 mins - Serves 4

INGREDIENTS

- 390g jar cherries in kirsch
- 2 tbsp dark brown sugar
- 4 big scoops of vanilla ice cream
- 50g amaretti biscuits

DIRECTIONS

STEP 1

Tip the cherries and sugar into a small saucepan. Bring to a simmer over a medium heat, stirring, and allow to bubble for 10 mins. Leave to cool slightly.

STEP 2

Scoop the ice cream into four bowls and pour over the warm compote. Crumble over the amaretti and serve.

HARISSA-CRUMBED FISH WITH LENTILS & PEPPERS

Prep: 15 mins - Cook: 15 mins |Serves 4

INGREDIENTS

- 2 x 200g pouches cooked puy lentils
- 200g jar roasted red peppers , drained and torn into chunks
- 50g black olives , from a jar, roughly chopped
- 1 lemon , zested and cut into wedges
- 3 tbsp olive or rapeseed oil
- 4 x 140g cod fillets (or another white fish)
- 100g fresh breadcrumbs
- 1 tbsp harissa
- ½ small pack flat-leaf parsley , chopped

DIRECTIONS

STEP 1

Heat oven to 200C/180C fan/gas 6. Mix the lentils, peppers, olives, lemon zest, 2 tbsp oil and some seasoning in a roasting tin. Top with the fish fillets. Mix the breadcrumbs, harissa and the remaining oil and put a few spoonfuls on top of each piece of fish. Bake for 12-15 mins until the fish is cooked, the topping is crispy and the lentils are hot. Scatter with the parsley and squeeze over the lemon wedges.

CRISPY ASIAN SALMON WITH STIR-FRIED NOODLES, PAK CHOI & SUGAR SNAP PEAS

Prep: 10 mins - Cook: 15 mins - Serves 2

INGREDIENTS

- 2 x 100g salmon fillets (plus 2 more 100g salmon fillets if cooking for Flaked salmon salad lunch - see 'goes well with')
- For the marinade
- 2 tsp reduced salt tamari or soy sauce
- 2cm piece ginger, peeled and finely chopped or grated
- 1 garlic clove, finely chopped
- 2 tbsp lemon or lime juice
- 1 tsp sesame oil
- For the stir-fried noodles
- 85g vermicelli rice noodle
- 2 tsp rapeseed oil
- 1 tsp sesame oil
- 1 spring onion, trimmed and thinly sliced

- 1 garlic clove, finely chopped
- ½ red chilli, deseeded and finely chopped
- 2cm piece ginger, peeled and finely chopped
- 100g sugar snap pea
- 100g pak choi (or spinach)
- 1 large red pepper, sliced
- 1 tsp tamari or soy sauce
- 1 tsp Thai fish sauce
- juice ½ lime
- 1 tbsp finely chopped coriander

DIRECTIONS

STEP 1

Make the marinade by mixing together all the ingredients. Place the salmon fillets in a small bowl and spoon over the marinade, turning the fish so that it's nicely coated. Cover with cling film and leave to sit for 10 mins (or longer if you have time).

STEP 2

Meanwhile, cook the noodles following pack instructions, then drain and sit them in a bowl of cold water.

STEP 3

Heat a non-stick frying pan. Add the salmon fillets, skin-side down, and leave for 3 mins. When the fish is slightly crispy, flip over and cook for a further 3 mins on the other side. Just before you remove the fish from the pan, add any remaining marinade and let it sizzle for 10 secs. Place 2 of the fillets, skin-side up, with their juices on a plate and cover with foil to keep warm. Put the other 2 fillets on another plate if using for Flaked salmon salad (see 'goes well with'), cover with foil, leave to cool, then chill.

STEP 4

In a frying pan or wok, heat the rapeseed and sesame oils over a high heat. Add the spring onion, garlic, chilli and ginger, and stir constantly for about 1 min. Add the sugar snap peas, pak choi and pepper, and stir for another 1-2 mins, then add the cooked noodles. Toss well, then add the soy sauce, fish sauce and lime juice, and mix until well combined and the pan is sizzling.

STEP 5

Remove from the heat and divide between 2 bowls. Top each with a salmon fillet and drizzle over any juices. Sprinkle with coriander and serve.

SQUASH & SPINACH FUSILLI WITH PECANS

Prep: 10 mins - Cook: 40 mins - Serves 2

INGREDIENTS

- 160g butternut squash , diced
- 3 garlic cloves , sliced
- 1 tbsp chopped sage leaves
- 2 tsp rapeseed oil
- 1 large courgette , halved and sliced
- 6 pecan halves
- 115g wholemeal fusilli
- 125g bag baby spinach

DIRECTIONS

STEP 1

Heat oven to 200C/180C fan/gas 6. Toss the butternut squash, garlic and sage in the oil, then spread out in a roasting tin and cook in the oven for 20 mins, add the courgettes and cook for a further 15 mins. Give everything a stir, then add the pecans and cook for 5 mins more until the nuts are toasted and the vegetables are tender and starting to caramelise.

STEP 2

Meanwhile, boil the pasta according to pack instructions – about 12 mins. Drain, then tip into a serving bowl and toss with the spinach so that it wilts in the heat from the pasta. Add the roasted veg and pecans, breaking up the nuts a little, and toss again really well before serving.

SALI MURGHI

Prep: 20 mins - Cook: 55 mins - Serves 6 - 8

INGREDIENTS

- 2½ tbsp ghee or vegetable oil
- 8 chicken thighs
- 1 cinnamon stick
- 5 green cardamom pods , bashed, seeds removed

- 1 tsp cumin seeds
- 2 onions , finely chopped
- 2 green chillies , roughly chopped
- 3 garlic cloves , roughly chopped
- 5cm piece ginger , roughly chopped
- 1 tsp ground coriander
- 1 tsp ground garam masala
- 1 tsp Kashmiri chilli powder
- ½ tsp turmeric
- 3 medium tomatoes , around 300g, finely chopped (or blitzed)
- 2 tbsp white wine vinegar
- 2 tsp jaggery (or soft brown sugar)
- 150g dried apricots (use the soft, ready-to-eat type)
- ½ small pack coriander , chopped
- Sali (optional)
- 1 large potato , peeled and sliced into matchsticks (see tip below)
- vegetable oil , for shallow frying

DIRECTIONS

STEP 1

Melt 1 tbsp of the ghee in a pan and add the chicken, skin-side side down. Once the skin is golden and crisp (around 5 mins), remove from the pan and set aside (you may need to do this in batches). Melt the remaining ghee in the pan, add the cinnamon, cardamom and cumin seeds, and fry until fragrant – around 5 mins. Stir in the onions along with a big pinch of salt and fry for 5 mins until browning in places.

STEP 2

Blitz the green chilli with the garlic and ginger, add to the pan and cook for 2 more mins, then stir in the spices and cook for a few mins more, splashing in a little water to prevent the spices from sticking. Tip in the chopped tomatoes.

STEP 3

Return the chicken to the pan, coating it with the curry base, then splash in the white wine vinegar followed by the jaggery. Add 100ml water, then cover and simmer for 30 mins. Remove the lid and stir in the apricots and coriander, then cook for 10-15 mins longer, until the gravy reduces.

STEP 4

Meanwhile, make the sali. Pat the potato matchsticks dry with kitchen paper. Pour vegetable oil into a small, deep saucepan until it's a few cm deep, and heat over a medium-high heat. Add a handful of the potato matchsticks at a time and fry for around a minute, until golden and crisp. Remove with a slotted spoon, drain on kitchen paper and season generously. Serve the curry with the sali piled on top.

ASPARAGUS & LEMON SPAGHETTI WITH PEAS

Prep: 7 mins - Cook: 12 mins - Serves 2

INGREDIENTS

- 150g wholemeal spaghetti
- 160g asparagus, ends trimmed and cut into lengths
- 2 tbsp rapeseed oil
- 2 leeks (220g), cut into lengths, then thin strips
- 1 red chilli, deseeded and finely chopped
- 1 garlic clove, finely grated
- 160g frozen peas
- 1 lemon, zested and juiced, plus wedges to serve

DIRECTIONS

STEP 1

Boil the spaghetti for 12 mins until al dente, adding the asparagus for the last 3 mins. Meanwhile, heat the oil in a large non-stick frying pan, add the leeks and chilli and cook for 5 mins. Stir in the garlic, peas and lemon zest and juice and cook for a few mins more.

STEP 2

Drain and add the pasta to the pan with ¼ mug of the pasta water and toss everything together until well mixed. Spoon into shallow bowls and serve with lemon wedges for squeezing over, if you like.

COURGETTE, LEEK & GOAT'S CHEESE SOUP

Prep: 8 mins - Cook: 17 mins - Serves 4

INGREDIENTS

- 1 tbsp rapeseed oil

* 400g leeks, well washed and sliced
* 450g courgettes, sliced
* 3 tsp vegetable bouillon powder, made up to 1 litre with boiling water
* 400g spinach
* 150g tub soft vegetarian goat's cheese
* 15g basil, plus a few leaves to serve
* 8 tsp omega seed mix (see tip)
* 4 x 25g portions wholegrain rye bread

DIRECTIONS

STEP 1

Heat the oil in a large pan and fry the leeks for a few mins to soften. Add the courgettes, then cover the pan and cook for 5 mins more. Pour in the stock, cover and cook for about 7 mins.

STEP 2

Add the spinach, then cover the pan and cook for 5 mins so that it wilts. Take off the heat and blitz until really smooth with a hand blender. Add the goat's cheese and basil, then blitz again.

STEP 3

If you're making this recipe as part of our two-person Summer Healthy Diet Plan, spoon half the soup into two bowls or large flasks, then cool and chill the remainder for another day. Reheat in a pan or microwave to serve. If serving in bowls, scatter with some extra basil leaves and the seeds, and eat with the rye bread.

LOW-FAT MOUSSAKA

Prep: 15 mins - Cook: 40 mins - Serves 4

INGREDIENTS

* 200g frozen sliced peppers
* 3 garlic cloves , crushed
* 200g extra-lean minced beef
* 100g red lentils
* 2 tsp dried oregano , plus extra for sprinkling
* 500ml carton passata
* 1 aubergine , sliced into 1.5cm rounds
* 4 tomatoes , sliced into 1cm rounds
* 2 tsp olive oil

- 25g parmesan , finely grated
- 170g pot 0% fat Greek yogurt
- freshly grated nutmeg

DIRECTIONS

STEP 1

Cook the peppers gently in a large non-stick pan for about 5 mins – the water from them should stop them sticking. Add the garlic and cook for 1 min more, then add the beef, breaking up with a fork, and cook until brown. Tip in the lentils, half the oregano, the passata and a splash of water. Simmer for 15-20 mins until the lentils are tender, adding more water if you need to.

STEP 2

Meanwhile, heat the grill to Medium. Arrange the aubergine and tomato slices on a non-stick baking tray and brush with the oil. Sprinkle with the remaining oregano and some seasoning, then grill for 1-2 mins each side until lightly charred – you may need to do this in batches.

STEP 3

Mix half the Parmesan with the yogurt and some seasoning. Divide the beef mixture between 4 small ovenproof dishes and top with the sliced aubergine and tomato. Spoon over the yogurt topping and sprinkle with the extra oregano, Parmesan and nutmeg. Grill for 3-4 mins until bubbling. Serve with a salad, if you like.

SALMON SALAD WITH SESAME DRESSING

Prep: 7 mins - Cook: 16 mins - Serves 2

INGREDIENTS

For the salad

- 250g new potatoes , sliced
- 160g French beans , trimmed
- 2 wild salmon fillets
- 80g salad leaves
- 4 small clementines , 3 sliced, 1 juiced
- handful of basil , chopped
- handful of coriander , chopped

For the dressing

- 2 tsp sesame oil
- 2 tsp tamari
- ½ lemon , juiced
- 1 red chilli , deseeded and chopped
- 2 tbsp finely chopped onion (1/4 small onion)

DIRECTIONS

STEP 1

Steam the potatoes and beans in a steamer basket set over a pan of boiling water for 8 mins. Arrange the salmon fillets on top and steam for a further 6-8 mins, or until the salmon flakes easily when tested with a fork.

STEP 2

Meanwhile, mix the dressing ingredients together along with the clementine juice. If eating straightaway, divide the salad leaves between two plates and top with the warm potatoes and beans and the clementine slices. Arrange the salmon fillets on top, scatter over the herbs and spoon over the dressing. If taking to work, prepare the potatoes, beans and salmon the night before, then pack into a rigid airtight container with the salad leaves kept separate. Put the salad elements together and dress just before eating to prevent the leaves from wilting.

COD WITH CUCUMBER, AVOCADO & MANGO SALSA SALAD

Prep: 5 mins - Cook: 8 mins - Serves 2

INGREDIENTS

- 2 x skinless cod fillets
- 1 lime , zested and juiced
- 1 small mango , peeled, stoned and chopped (or 2 peaches, stoned and chopped)
- 1 small avocado , stoned, peeled and sliced
- ¼ cucumber , chopped
- 160g cherry tomatoes , quartered
- 1 red chilli , deseeded and chopped
- 2 spring onions , sliced
- handful chopped coriander

DIRECTIONS

STEP 1

Heat oven to 200C/180C fan/gas 6. Put the fish in a shallow ovenproof dish and pour over half the lime juice, with a little of the zest, then grind over some black pepper. Bake for 8 mins or until the fish flakes easily but is still moist.

STEP 2

Meanwhile, put the rest of the ingredients, plus the remaining lime juice and zest, in a bowl and combine well. Spoon onto plates and top with the cod, spooning over any juices in the dish.

EASTER BISCUITS

Prep: 1 hr and 15 mins - Cook: 30 mins - makes 18

INGREDIENTS

- 300g plain flour , plus extra for dusting
- 150g white caster sugar
- 150g slightly salted butter , chopped
- 1 large egg
- 2 tsp vanilla extract or vanilla bean paste

For the iced option

- 500g royal icing sugar
- your favourite food colouring gels
- For the jammy middle option
- icing sugar , for dusting
- 400g apricot jam , or lemon curd

DIRECTIONS

STEP 1

Weigh the flour and sugar in a bowl. Add the butter and rub together with your fingertips until the mixture resembles wet sand, with no buttery lumps. Beat the egg with the vanilla, then add to the bowl. Mix briefly with a cutlery knife to combine, then use your hands to knead the dough together – try not to overwork the dough, or the biscuits will be tough. Shape into a disc, then wrap in cling film and chill for at least 15 mins. Heat oven to 180C/160C fan/gas 4. Line two baking sheets with baking parchment.

STEP 2

Dust a work surface with flour. Halve the dough, then roll one half out to the thickness of a £1 coin. Use an egg-shaped cookie cutter (ours was 10cm long; you could also make a cardboard template to cut around) to stamp out as many cookies as you can, then transfer them to one of the baking sheets, leaving a little space between the biscuits. Repeat with the other half of the dough. If you want to make jammy biscuits, use a small circular cutter to stamp holes in half of the biscuits (where the yolk would be). If you intend to make both iced and jammy biscuits, only stamp holes in a quarter of the biscuits.

STEP 3

Bake for 12-15 mins, until the biscuits are pale gold. Cool on the sheets for 10 mins, then transfer to a wire rack to cool fully. Once cool, decorate to your liking (see next **STEP**s). Will keep in an airtight container for up to five days.

STEP 4

To decorate the biscuits with icing, add enough water to the icing sugar to make a thick icing – it should hold its shape without spreading when piped. Transfer about a third of the icing to a piping bag fitted with a very small round nozzle (or just snip a tiny opening at the tip). Pipe an outline around the biscuits, then draw patterns in the middle – lines, spots and zigzags work well. Leave to dry for 10 mins. Divide the remaining icing between as many colours as you'd like to use, then use the gels to dye them. Loosen each icing with a few drops of water, then transfer them to piping bags. Use the coloured icing to fill the empty spaces on the biscuits. You may need to use a cocktail stick to tease it into the corners. Once covered, leave to dry for a few hours.

STEP 5

To make the jammy middle biscuits, dust the biscuits with holes in the middle with a heavy coating of icing sugar. Spread the jam or curd generously over the whole biscuits, then sandwich the dusted biscuits on top of them.

GINGER CHICKEN & GREEN BEAN NOODLES

Prep: 10 mins - Cook: 15 mins - Serves 2

INGREDIENTS

- ½ tbsp vegetable oil
- 2 skinless chicken breasts, sliced
- 200g green beans , trimmed and halved crosswise
- thumb-sized piece of ginger , peeled and cut into matchsticks

- 2 garlic cloves , sliced
- 1 ball stem ginger , finely sliced, plus 1 tsp syrup from the jar
- 1 tsp cornflour , mixed with 1 tbsp water
- 1 tsp dark soy sauce , plus extra to serve (optional)
- 2 tsp rice vinegar
- 200g cooked egg noodles

DIRECTIONS

STEP 1

Heat the oil in a wok over a high heat and stir-fry the chicken for 5 mins. Add the green beans and stir-fry for 4-5 mins more until the green beans are just tender, and the chicken is just cooked through.

STEP 2

Stir in the fresh ginger and garlic, and stir-fry for 2 mins, then add the stem ginger and syrup, the cornflour mix, soy sauce and vinegar. Stir-fry for 1 min, then toss in the noodles. Cook until everything is hot and the sauce coats the noodles. Drizzle with more soy, if you like, and serve.

POTATO, PEA & EGG CURRY ROTIS

Prep: 5 mins - Cook: 25 mins - Serves 4

INGREDIENTS

- 1 tbsp oil
- 2 tbsp mild curry paste
- 400g can chopped tomatoes
- 2 potatoes , cut into small chunks
- 200g peas
- 3 eggs , hard-boiled
- pack rotis , warmed through
- 150g tub natural yogurt , to serve

DIRECTIONS

STEP 1

Heat the oil in a saucepan and briefly fry the curry paste. Tip in the tomatoes and half a can of water and bring to a simmer. Add the potatoes and cook for 20 mins, or until the potato is tender. Stir in the peas and cook for 3 mins.

Halve the eggs and place them on top of the curry, then warm everything through. Serve with the rotis and yogurt on the side.

ALL-IN–ONE CHICKEN WITH WILTED SPINACH

Prep: 20 mins - Cook: 1 hr - Serves 2

INGREDIENTS

- 2 beetroot , peeled and cut into small chunks
- 300g celeriac , cut into small chunks
- 2 red onions , quartered
- 8 garlic cloves , 4 crushed, the rest left whole, but peeled
- 1 tbsp rapeseed oil
- 1½ tbsp fresh thyme leaves , plus extra to serve
- 1 lemon , zested and juiced
- 1 tsp fennel seeds
- 1 tsp English mustard powder
- 1 tsp smoked paprika
- 4 tbsp bio yogurt
- 4 bone-in chicken thighs , skin removed
- 260g bag spinach

DIRECTIONS

STEP 1

Heat oven to 200C/180C fan/gas 6. Tip the beetroot, celeriac, onions and whole garlic cloves into a shallow roasting tin. Add the oil, 1 tbsp thyme, half the lemon zest, fennel seeds and a squeeze of lemon juice, then toss together. Roast for 20 mins while you prepare the chicken.

STEP 2

Stir the mustard powder and paprika into 2 tbsp yogurt in a bowl. Add half the crushed garlic, the remaining lemon zest and thyme, and juice from half the lemon. Add the chicken and toss well until it's coated all over. Put the chicken in the tin with the veg and roast for 40 mins until the chicken is cooked through and the vegetables are tender.

STEP 3

About 5 mins before the chicken is ready, wash and drain the spinach and put it in a pan with the remaining crushed garlic. Cook until wilted, then turn off the heat and stir in the remaining yogurt. Scatter some extra thyme over the chicken and vegetables, then serve.

APPLE & ALMOND CAKE

Prep: 10 mins - Cook: 35 mins - 40 mins - Serves 8

INGREDIENTS

- 125ml (½ cup) olive oil
- 140g (½ cup) maple syrup or agave syrup
- 2 eggs
- 130g (1/2 cup) apple sauce (shop-bought or homemade)
- 185g (2 cups) ground almonds
- 1 tsp baking powder
- 1 tsp cinnamon

For the topping

- 1 apple , skin-on, cored and diced
- tiny splash olive oil
- 1 tbsp maple syrup
- ½ tsp cinnamon

DIRECTIONS

STEP 1

Heat oven to 190C/170C fan/gas 5, and lightly oil a 20cm springform tin and line the base with a circle of baking parchment.

STEP 2

In a stand mixer, or using a hand blender, whizz together the oil and maple syrup for 30 secs. Add the eggs and whizz for another 1 min before adding the apple sauce and blending for a further 30 secs. Tip in the ground almonds, baking powder, 1 tsp salt and cinnamon, blend for 30 secs and your batter is done. Pour it into the tin, and bake for around 30-40 mins or until the top is a deep golden brown, the cake is coming away from the sides a little, and a skewer inserted into the centre comes out clean.

STEP 3

While it's cooking, make the topping. In a small frying pan, cook the apple gently with the rest of the topping ingredients and ½ tsp salt until the apple is soft and gently caramelised. When the cake is ready, scatter the bronzed apple chunks on top of the cake. You could also make it with chunks of caramelised peach or plum on top, or some cherry compote, or any berries which you have softened in a pan with a little water and maple syrup. Eat warm, as a pudding, with a spoonful of Greek yogurt, or cold with a cup of tea or coffee.

EASY VEGAN PHO

Prep: 10 mins - Cook: 20 mins - Serves 2

INGREDIENTS

- 100g rice noodles
- 1 tsp Marmite
- 1 tsp vegetable oil
- 50g chestnut mushrooms , sliced
- 1 leek , sliced
- 2 tbsp soy sauce

To serve

- 1 red chilli , sliced (deseeded if you don't like it too hot)
- ½ bunch mint , leaves picked and stalk discarded
- handful salted peanuts
- sriracha , to serve

DIRECTIONS

STEP 1

Tip the noodles into a bowl and cover with boiling water. Leave to stand for 10 mins, then drain, rinse in cold water and set aside.

STEP 2

In a jug, mix the Marmite with 500ml boiling water. Set aside while you cook the vegetables.

STEP 3

Heat the oil in a saucepan, then add the mushrooms and leek. Cook for 10-15 mins until softened and beginning to colour, then add the soy sauce and Marmite and water mixture and stir. Bring to the boil for 5 mins.

Divide the noodles between two deep bowls, then ladle over the hot broth. Top with the chilli slices, mint leaves and peanuts, and serve with some sriracha on the side.

SEARED BEEF SALAD WITH CAPERS & MINT

Prep: 10 mins - Cook: 12 mins - Serves 2

INGREDIENTS

- 150g new potatoes , thickly sliced
- 160g fine green beans , trimmed and halved
- 160g frozen peas
- rapeseed oil , for brushing
- 200g lean fillet steak , trimmed of any fat
- 160g romaine lettuce , roughly torn into pieces

For the dressing

- 1 tbsp extra virgin olive oil
- 2 tsp cider vinegar
- ½ tsp English mustard powder
- 2 tbsp chopped mint
- 3 tbsp chopped basil
- 1 garlic clove , finely grated
- 1 tbsp capers

DIRECTIONS

STEP 1

Cook the potatoes in a pan of simmering water for 5 mins. Add the beans and cook 5 mins more, then tip in the peas and cook for 2 mins until all the vegetables are just tender. Drain.

STEP 2

Meanwhile, measure all the dressing ingredients in a large bowl and season with black pepper. Stir and crush the herbs and capers with the back of a spoon to intensify their flavours.

STEP 3

Brush a little oil over the steak and grind over some black pepper. Heat a non-stick frying pan over a high heat and cook the steak for 4 mins on one side and 2-3 mins on the other, depending on the thickness and how rare you like it. Transfer to a plate to rest while you carry on with the rest of the salad.

STEP 4

Mix the warm vegetables into the dressing until well coated, then add the lettuce and toss again. Pile onto plates. Slice the steak and turn in any dressing left in the bowl, add to the salad and serve while still warm.

MINTY GRIDDLED CHICKEN & PEACH SALAD

Prep: 10 mins - Cook: 15 mins - Serves 2

INGREDIENTS

- 1 lime , zested and juiced
- 1 tbsp rapeseed oil
- 2 tbsp mint , finely chopped, plus a few leaves to serve
- 1 garlic clove , finely grated
- 2 skinless chicken breast fillets (300g)
- 160g fine beans , trimmed and halved
- 2 peaches (200g), each cut into 8 thick wedges
- 1 red onion , cut into wedges
- 1 large Little Gem lettuce (165g), roughly shredded
- ½ x 60g pack rocket
- 1 small avocado , stoned and sliced
- 240g cooked new potatoes

DIRECTIONS

STEP 1

Mix the lime zest and juice, oil and mint, then put half in a bowl with the garlic. Thickly slice the chicken at a slight angle, add to the garlic mixture and toss together with plenty of black pepper.

STEP 2

Cook the beans in a pan of water for 3-4 mins until just tender. Meanwhile, griddle the chicken and onion for a few mins each side until cooked and tender. Transfer to a plate, then quickly griddle the peaches. If you don't have a griddle pan, use a non-stick frying pan with a drop of oil.

STEP 3

Toss the warm beans and onion in the remaining mint mixture, and pile onto a platter or into individual shallow bowls with the lettuce and rocket. Top with the avocado, peaches and chicken and scatter over the mint. Serve with the potatoes while still warm.

PARMA PORK WITH POTATO SALAD

Prep: 15 mins - Cook: 15 mins - Serves 2

INGREDIENTS

- 175g new potatoes (we used Jersey Royals), scrubbed and thickly sliced
- 3 celery sticks, thickly sliced
- 3 tbsp bio yogurt
- 2 gherkins (about 85g each), sliced
- ¼ tsp caraway seeds
- ½ tsp Dijon mustard
- 2 x 100g pieces lean pork tenderloin
- 2 tsp chopped sage
- 2 slices Parma ham
- 1 tsp rapeseed oil
- 2 tsp balsamic vinegar
- 2 handfuls salad leaves

DIRECTIONS

STEP 1

Bring a pan of water to the boil, add the potatoes and celery and cook for 8 mins. Meanwhile, mix the yogurt, guerkins, caraway and mustard in a bowl. When the potatoes and celery are cooked, drain and set aside for a few mins to cool a little.

STEP 2

Bash the pork pieces with a rolling pin to flatten them. Sprinkle over the sage and some pepper, then top each with a slice of Parma ham. Heat the oil in a non-stick pan, add the pork and cook for a couple of mins each side, turning carefully. Add the balsamic vinegar and let it sizzle in the pan.

STEP 3

Stir the potatoes and celery into the dressing and serve with the pork, with some salad leaves on the side.

LOW-SUGAR LIME & BASIL GREEN JUICE

Prep: 5 mins - no cook - Serves 1

INGREDIENTS

- 70ml chilled apple and elderflower juice
- 50g baby spinach
- 20g basil leaves
- 6cm piece of cucumber (about 100g), chopped
- 1 lime , zested and juiced

DIRECTIONS

STEP 1

Pour the apple juice into a large jug then add the spinach, basil, cucumber, lime and 100ml chilled water.

STEP 2

Blitz really well with a hand blender until very smooth. Pour into a glass and drink straightaway.

LOW-SUGAR GRANOLA

Prep: 10 mins - Cook: 30 mins - 35 mins - Makes 500g

INGREDIENTS

- 200g rolled oats
- 150g bag mixed nuts
- 150g mixed seeds
- 1 orange , zested
- 2 tsp mixed spice
- 2 tsp cinnamon
- 2 tbsp cold pressed rapeseed oil
- 1½ tbsp maple syrup

DIRECTIONS

STEP 1

Heat oven to 160C/140C fan/gas 4. Mix all the ingredients in a bowl with a pinch of salt, then spread out on a baking tray.

Roast for 30-35 mins until golden, pulling the tray out of the oven twice while cooking to give everything a good stir – this will help the granola toast evenly. Leave to cool. Will keep in an airtight container for one month.

LOW SUGAR CHOCOLATE SANDWICH CAKE

Prep: 35 mins - Cook: 25 mins - 30 mins |Cuts into 12

INGREDIENTS

For the cake

- 150ml rapeseed oil , plus extra for greasing
- 250g cooked beetroot
- 50g cocoa
- 140g plain wholewheat flour
- 100g plain white flour
- 50g ground almonds
- 200g xylitol , such as Total Sweet
- 2 tsp baking powder
- 1 tsp bicarbonate of soda
- 2 large eggs
- 2 tsp vanilla extract
- 50ml skimmed milk

For the chocolate cream

- 150ml pot natural bio-yogurt
- 2 tbsp cocoa
- 100g xylitol such as Total Sweet
- 150ml pot double cream

DIRECTIONS

STEP 1

Heat oven to 160C/140C/gas 3 and grease then line the base of two x 20cm sandwich tins with baking parchment. To start making the chocolate cream stir the yogurt with the cocoa and xylitol until completely blended then set aside while you make the cake. This helps to dissolve the xylitol granules.

STEP 2

To make the cake, first blitz the beetroot in a food processor until it resembles a thick puree. Tip in the cocoa, flours, ground almonds, xylitol, baking powder and soda and pulse briefly to mix the ingredients together.

STEP 3

Now add the eggs, the 150ml rapeseed oil, vanilla extract and milk, and blitz again to make a smooth liquid batter.

STEP 4

Divide the mixture evenly between the tins working quickly, as the baking powder activates once in contact with the liquid ingredients, then bake for 25-30 mins until a skewer poked into the middle of the cake comes out clean. Cool for few mins then remove from the tins and finish cooling on a wire rack. Once cold, carefully strip off the lining paper.

STEP 5

To finish the chocolate cream, whip the double cream until it holds its shape. Stir the cocoa mixture then fold in all but 2 tsp. Spread a third on top of one of the cold sponge cakes, top with the remaining sponge and spread with the rest of the chocolate cream to create a swirly finish. Dot over the reserved cocoa mixture and gently feather in with the end of a teaspoon. The cake will keep in the fridge for a couple of days, but return to room temperature before eating for the best taste and texture.

LOW-SUGAR MARMALADE

Prep: 30 mins - 45 mins - Cook: 1 hr |Makes about 2.25kg/5lb

INGREDIENTS

- 900g Seville orange
- 600ml pure, unsweetened apple juice
- 900g jam sugar (available in all large supermarkets)

DIRECTIONS

STEP 1

Cut the oranges into thin slices. Remove the pips and tie them in a muslin bag. Place the orange slices in a preserving pan with the apple juice and the pips. Bring to the boil then simmer very gently for 30-40 minutes, or until the orange peel can be pierced easily with a fork. The mixture will be very thick, with little liquid.

STEP 2

Add the jam sugar and stir over a low heat until it has completely dissolved, about 5 minutes. Bring to a good rolling boil then bubble for 4 minutes. Take the pan off the heat and skim any scum from the surface. (To dissolve any excess scum, drop a small knob of butter on to the surface, and gently stir.)

STEP 3

Remove the muslin bag and leave the marmalade to stand in the pan for 15 minutes to cool a little, and to allow the peel to settle; pot in sterilised jars, seal and label.

PEACH GALETTE WITH BROWN SUGAR CRUST

Prep: 30 mins - Cook: 35 mins plus chilling - Serves 8

INGREDIENTS

- 50g salted butter , softened
- 50g light brown soft sugar
- 1 medium egg
- 100g ground almonds
- 5-6 peaches or nectarines
- ½ lemon , juiced
- 1 tbsp cornflour
- 1 tsp vanilla bean paste or extract
- 3 tbsp icing sugar
- 2 tbsp peach jam
- thick double cream or vanilla ice cream, to serve

For the pastry

- 250g plain flour , plus more to dust
- 200g cold butter , diced
- 65g light brown soft sugar
- 2 eggs , 1 yolk only (freeze the white for another recipe), 1 whole egg beaten to glaze

- 2 tbsp demerara sugar , for sprinkling

DIRECTIONS

STEP 1

To make the pastry, put the flour, butter and sugar in the bowl of food processor and pulse until it looks like breadcrumbs. Add the egg yolk and 1 tbsp cold water, then pulse again until it forms a ball. Wrap and chill for 30 mins.

STEP 2

For the frangipane, beat the butter and sugar together until pale and fluffy, add the egg, whisk again, then fold in the ground almonds to make a paste. Cut the peaches into thin slices, then toss in a bowl with the lemon juice, cornflour, vanilla and icing sugar. Mix gently until the fruit is coated and the cornflour dissolved. Heat the oven to 200C/180C fan/gas 6 and heat a large baking sheet on the middle shelf.

STEP 3

Roll the pastry out in between two pieces of baking parchment to a large disc about 5mm thick and 35cm in diameter. Remove the top layer of parchment, draw a 30cm circle onto it, cut it out, and use as a template to cut out a disc of pastry, or roughly trim the pastry into a circle by eye for a more rustic look.

STEP 4

Smooth the frangipane over the middle of the pastry with a spatula, leaving a 5cm border around the edge. Arrange the peach slices over the top in a pattern, either in a circle or little fans of fruit.

STEP 5

Fold in the edges of the pastry to slightly overlap the fruit. Brush with the beaten egg and sprinkle over the demerara, then transfer to the hot baking sheet using the parchment.

STEP 6

Bake for 30-35 mins until the pastry is golden and the fruit looks soft. Leave to cool to room temperature. Heat the jam in the microwave for a few seconds, or in a small pan until warm and runny, then use to glaze the fruit. Serve with thick cream or ice cream.

MUSHROOM STROGANOFF

Prep: 10 mins - Cook: 20 mins - Serves 2

INGREDIENTS

- 2 tsp olive oil
- 1 onion, finely chopped
- 1 tbsp paprika
- 2 garlic cloves, crushed
- 300g mixed mushrooms, chopped
- 150ml low-sodium beef or vegetable stock
- 1 tbsp Worcestershire sauce, or vegetarian alternative
- 3 tbsp half-fat soured cream
- small bunch of parsley, roughly chopped
- 250g pouch cooked wild rice

DIRECTIONS

STEP 1

Heat the olive oil in a large non-stick frying pan and soften the onion for about 5 mins.

STEP 2

Add the paprika and garlic, then cook for 1 min more. Add the mushrooms and cook on a high heat, stirring often, for about 5 mins.

STEP 3

Pour in the stock and Worcestershire sauce. Bring to the boil, bubble for 5 mins until the sauce thickens, then turn off the heat and stir through the soured cream and most of the parsley. Make sure the pan is not on the heat or the sauce may split.

STEP 4

Heat the wild rice following pack instructions, then stir through the remaining chopped parsley and serve with the stroganoff.

20-MINUTE SEAFOOD PASTA

Total time 20 mins - Ready in 20 mins - Serves 4

INGREDIENTS

- 1 tbsp olive oil
- 1 onion, chopped
- 1 garlic clove, chopped
- 1 tsp paprika

- 400g can chopped tomatoes
- 1l chicken stock (from a cube is fine)
- 300g spaghetti, roughly broken
- 240g frozen seafood mix, defrosted
- handful of parsley leaves, chopped, and lemon wedges, to serve

DIRECTIONS

STEP 1

Heat the oil in a wok or large frying pan, then cook the onion and garlic over a medium heat for 5 mins until soft. Add the paprika, tomatoes and stock, then bring to the boil.

STEP 2

Turn down the heat to a simmer, stir in the pasta and cook for 7 mins, stirring occasionally to stop the pasta from sticking. Stir in the seafood, cook for 3 mins more until it's all heated through and the pasta is cooked, then season to taste. Sprinkle with the parsley and serve with lemon wedges.

WATERMELON, LIME AND MINT SUGAR PAVLOVA

Prep: 30 mins - Cook: 1 hr and 15 mins plus at least 2 hrs cooling - Serves 10-12

INGREDIENTS

- ½ lemon , juiced (reserve the other half)
- 6 large egg whites
- 350g caster sugar
- 2 tsp cornflour
- 1 tsp vanilla extract

For the topping

- handful of mint leaves , plus extra to serve
- 50g caster sugar
- 400ml double cream
- 200g natural yogurt
- 1 lime , zested
- small watermelon , cut into wedges and rind removed

DIRECTIONS

STEP 1

Line a large baking sheet with baking parchment. Using an 18cm round cake tin or plate as a guide, draw a circle on the parchment, then flip it over. Heat the oven to 130C/110C fan/gas ½.

STEP 2

Rub the reserved lemon half around the inside of a large bowl or stand mixer, then wipe with kitchen paper to remove any butter or oil. Tip in the egg whites and whisk with an electric whisk or the mixer on a low speed until the whites form small, foamy bubbles, about 1-2 mins. Keep going until the mix looks like shaving foam, then add the sugar, 1 tbsp at a time, until it's a thick, glossy meringue. Rub some between your fingers – if you can feel any grains of sugar, keep whisking for a few minutes. Add the cornflour, lemon juice and vanilla, and whisk for another 30 seconds.

STEP 3

Spoon the meringue onto the prepared baking sheet, into the centre of the circle, and spread it out to the edges with a palette knife. Swipe the knife around the edge, then smooth the top.

STEP 4

Bake for 1 hr 15 mins, then turn the oven down to 100C/80C fan/gas ¼ and bake for 1 hr. Turn the oven off and leave the pavlova inside to cool for at least 2 hrs, or overnight.

STEP 5

Carefully invert the pavlova and peel away the parchment. Don't worry if it cracks a little – it will be covered by the topping.

STEP 6

To make the topping, blitz the mint with the caster sugar. Whisk the double cream and natural yogurt with an electric whisk until just holding its shape. Sprinkle over the lime zest and mint sugar, then fold into the cream mix with a large metal spoon to ripple. Spoon over the pavlova. Top with the rest of the mint sugar, the watermelon and more mint. Serve with lime wedges to squeeze over. Best served straightaway but leftovers will keep in the fridge for two days.

VEGAN PIZZA MARGHERITA

Prep: 15 mins - Cook: 15 mins plus rising and proving - Makes 2 large or 4 small pizzas (serves 4)

INGREDIENTS

For the pizza dough

- 500g strong white bread flour, plus extra for dusting
- 1 tsp dried yeast
- 1 tsp caster sugar
- 1 ½ tbsp olive oil, plus extra

For the tomato sauce

- 100ml passata
- 1 tbsp fresh basil, chopped (or 1/2 tsp dried oregano)
- 1 garlic clove, crushed

For the topping

- 200g vegan mozzarella-style cheese, grated
- 2 tomatoes, thinly sliced
- Fresh basil or oregano leaves, chilli oil and vegan parmesan to serve (optional)

DIRECTIONS

STEP 1

Put the flour, yeast and sugar in a large bowl. Measure 150ml of cold water and 150ml boiling water into a jug and mix them together – this will mean your water is a good temperature for the yeast. Add the oil and 1 tsp salt to the warm water then pour it over the flour. Stir well with a spoon then start to knead the mixture together in the bowl until it forms a soft and slightly sticky dough. If it's too dry add a splash of cold water.

STEP 2

Dust a little flour on the work surface and knead the dough for 10 mins. Put it back in the mixing bowl and cover with cling film greased with a few drops of olive oil. Leave to rise in a warm place for 1 hr or until doubled in size.

STEP 3

Heat oven to 220C/200C/gas 9 and put a baking sheet or pizza stone on the top shelf to heat up. Once the dough has risen, knock it back by punching it a couple of times with your fist then kneading it again on a floured surface. It should be springy and a lot less sticky. Set aside while you prepare the sauce.

STEP 4

Put all the ingredients for the tomato sauce together in a bowl, season with salt, pepper and a pinch of sugar if you like and mix well. Set aside until needed.

STEP 5

Divide the dough into 2 or 4 pieces (depending on whether you want to make large or small pizzas), shape into balls and flatten each piece out as thin as you can get it with a rolling pin or using your hands. Make sure the dough is well dusted with flour to stop it sticking. Dust another baking sheet with flour then put a pizza base on top – spread 4-5 tbsp of the tomato sauce on top and add some sliced tomatoes and grated vegan cheese. Drizzle with a little olive oil and bake in the oven on top of your preheated baking tray for 10-12 mins or until the base is puffed up and the vegan cheese has melted and is bubbling and golden in patches.

STEP 6

Repeat with the rest of the dough and topping. Serve the pizzas with fresh basil leaves or chilli oil if you like and sprinkle over vegan parmesan just after baking.

BROCCOLI PASTA SHELLS

Prep: 5 mins - Cook: 15 mins - Serves 4

INGREDIENTS

- 1 head of broccoli, chopped into florets
- 1 garlic clove, unpeeled
- 2 tbsp olive oil
- 250g pasta shells
- ½ small pack parsley
- ½ small pack basil
- 30g toasted pine nuts
- ½ lemon, zested and juiced
- 30g parmesan (or vegetarian alternative), plus extra to serve

DIRECTIONS

STEP 1

Heat the oven to 200C/180C fan/gas 6. Toss the broccoli and garlic in 1 tbsp of the olive oil on a roasting tray and roast in the oven for 10-12 mins, until softened.

STEP 2

Tip the pasta shells into a pan of boiling, salted water. Cook according to packet instructions and drain. Tip the parsley, basil, pine nuts, lemon juice and parmesan into a blender. Once the broccoli is done, set aside a few of the smaller pieces. Squeeze the garlic from its skin, add to the blender along with the rest of the broccoli, pulse to a pesto and season well.

STEP 3

Toss the pasta with the pesto. Add the reserved broccoli florets, split between two bowls and top with a little extra parmesan, the lemon zest and a good grinding of black pepper, if you like.

CHILLI CHICKEN WRAPS

Prep: 10 mins - Cook: 25 mins - Serves 4

INGREDIENTS

- 2 tbsp vegetable oil
- 6 boneless, skinless chicken thighs, cut into bite-sized pieces
- 1 large onion, thinly sliced into half-moons
- 2 garlic cloves, finely chopped
- 3cm piece ginger, peeled and finely chopped
- ½ tsp ground cumin
- ½ tsp garam masala
- 1 tbsp tomato purée
- 1 red chilli, thinly sliced into rings
- juice ½ lemon
- 4 rotis, warmed
- ½ small red onion, chopped
- 4 tbsp mango chutney or lime pickle
- 4 handfuls mint or coriander
- 4 tbsp yogurt

DIRECTIONS

STEP 1

Heat the oil in a large frying pan over a medium heat. Add the chicken, brown on all sides, then remove. Add the onion, garlic, ginger and a pinch of salt. Cook for 5 mins or until softened.

STEP 2

Increase the heat to high. Return the chicken to the pan with the spices, tomato purée, chilli and lemon juice. Season well and cook for 10 mins or until the chicken is tender.

STEP 3

Divide the chicken, red onion, chutney, herbs and yogurt between the four warm rotis. Roll up and serve with plenty of napkins

SUGAR-CRUSTED BARA BRITH

Prep: 15 mins - Cook: 1 hr - 1 hr and 15 mins Plus overnight soaking - Serves 12

INGREDIENTS

- 400g/14oz luxury mixed fruit
- 75g pack dried cranberries
- mug hot strong black tea
- 100g butter , plus extra for greasing
- 2 heaped tbsp orange marmalade
- 2 eggs , beaten
- 450g self-raising flour - try a mix of wholemeal and white
- 175g light soft brown sugar
- 1 tsp each ground cinnamon and ground ginger
- 4 tbsp milk
- 50g crushed sugar cubes or granulated sugar, to decorate

DIRECTIONS

STEP 1

Mix together the dried fruit and cranberries in a large bowl, then pour the hot tea over. Cover with cling film and leave to soak overnight.

STEP 2

Heat oven to 180C/fan 160C/gas 4. Butter and line the bottom of a 900g/2lb loaf tin with baking parchment. Melt butter and marmalade together in a pan. Leave to cool for 5 mins, then beat in the eggs. Drain any excess tea from the fruit. Mix the flour, sugar and spices together, then stir in the fruit, butter mix and milk until evenly combined. The batter should softly drop from the spoon – add more milk if needed.

STEP 3

Spoon into the tin and level the top. Sprinkle with the crushed sugar and bake for 1-1¼ hrs until dark golden and a skewer inserted comes out clean. Cover loosely with foil if it starts to over-colour before the middle is cooked. Leave to cool completely in the tin and serve sliced.

THAI PRAWN & GINGER NOODLES

Prep: 15 mins - Cook: 15 mins plus soaking - Serves 2

INGREDIENTS

- 100g folded rice noodles (sen lek)
- zest and juice 1 small orange
- 1½-2 tbsp red curry paste
- 1-2 tsp fish sauce
- 2 tsp light brown soft sugar
- 1 tbsp sunflower oil
- 25g ginger, scraped and shredded
- 2 large garlic cloves, sliced
- 1 red pepper, deseeded and sliced
- 85g sugar snap peas, halved lengthways
- 140g beansprouts
- 175g pack raw king prawns
- handful chopped basil
- handful chopped coriander

DIRECTIONS

STEP 1

Put the noodles in a bowl and pour over boiling water to cover them. Set aside to soak for 10 mins. Stir together the orange juice and zest, curry paste, fish sauce, sugar and 3 tbsp water to make a sauce.

STEP 2

Heat the oil in a large wok and add half the ginger and the garlic. Cook, stirring, for 1 min. Add the pepper and stir-fry for 3 mins more. Toss in the sugar snaps, cook briefly, then pour in the curry sauce. Add the beansprouts and prawns, and continue cooking until the prawns just turn pink. Drain the noodles, then toss these into the pan with the herbs and remaining ginger. Mix until the noodles are well coated in the sauce, then serve.

EASY SOUP MAKER LENTIL SOUP

Prep: 5 mins - Cook: 30 mins - Serves 4

INGREDIENTS

- 750ml vegetable or ham stock
- 75g red lentils
- 3 carrots , finely chopped
- 1 medium leek , sliced (150g)

* small handful chopped parsley , to serve

DIRECTIONS

STEP 1

Put the stock, lentils, carrots and leek into a soup maker, and press the 'chunky soup' function. Make sure you don't fill it above the max fill line. The soup will look a little foamy to start, but don't worry – it will disappear once cooked.

STEP 2

Once the cycle is complete, check the lentils are tender, and season well. Scatter over the parsley to serve.

FROSÉ

Prep: 5 mins(plus freezing overnight) - Serves 4-6

INGREDIENTS

* 1 bottle dry rosé
* 300g strawberries , hulled and halved
* 50g caster sugar
* juice of 1 lemon

DIRECTIONS

STEP 1

Pour the bottle of rosé into a deep roasting tin and carefully put it in the freezer overnight.

STEP 2

The next day, mix the strawberries with the sugar and leave to sit for 30 mins until the strawberries begin to release their juices.

STEP 3

Blend the frozen rosé, strawberries, sugar and lemon juice together, then divide between glasses for the ultimate refreshing summer cocktail.

ASIAN TOFU WITH STIR-FRIED NOODLES, PAK CHOI & SUGAR SNAP PEAS

Prep: 10 mins - Cook: 15 mins plus marinatingq - Serves 2

INGREDIENTS

* 195g extra-firm tofu

For the marinade

* 2 tsp tamari or soy sauce
* 2cm piece ginger , peeled and finely chopped or grated
* 1 garlic clove , finely chopped
* 2 tbsp lemon or lime juice
* 1 tsp sesame oil

For the stir-fried noodles

* 85g vermicelli rice noodle
* 2 tsp rapeseed oil
* 1 tsp sesame oil
* 1 spring onion , trimmed and thinly sliced
* 1 garlic clove , finely chopped
* ½ red chilli , deseeded and finely chopped
* 2cm piece ginger , peeled and finely chopped
* 100g sugar snap pea
* 100g pak choi (or spinach)
* 1 large red pepper , sliced
* 1 tsp tamari or soy sauce
* juice ½ lime
* 1 tbsp finely chopped coriander

DIRECTIONS

STEP 1

Make the marinade by mixing together all the INGREDIENTS. Drain the tofu by placing on several sheets of kitchen paper on a plate, with several more on top, and a heavy weight (such as a pan) on top of that. Leave for at least 15 mins. Cut the tofu into cubes and put in a small bowl with the marinade. Cover and leave for 30 mins-1 hr.

STEP 2

Meanwhile, cook the noodles following pack instructions, then drain and sit them in a bowl of cold water.

STEP 3

Heat a non-stick frying pan. Add the tofu pieces and fry until hot and crispy. Just before you remove the tofu from the pan, add any remaining marinade and let it sizzle for 10 secs. Place the tofu on a plate and cover with foil to keep warm.

STEP 4

In a frying pan or wok, heat the rapeseed and sesame oils over a high heat. Add the spring onion, garlic, chilli and ginger, and stir constantly for about 1 min. Add the sugar snap peas, pak choi and pepper, and stir for another 1-2 mins, then add the cooked noodles. Toss well, then add the soy sauce and lime juice, and mix until well combined and the pan is sizzling.

STEP 5

Remove from the heat and divide between 2 bowls. Top each with tofu cubes and drizzle over any juices. Sprinkle with coriander and serve.

MEXICAN PENNE WITH AVOCADO

Prep: 10 mins - Cook: 20 mins - Serves 2

INGREDIENTS

- 100g wholemeal penne
- 1 tsp rapeseed oil
- 1 large onion, sliced, plus 1 tbsp finely chopped
- 1 orange pepper, deseeded and cut into chunks
- 2 garlic cloves, grated
- 2 tsp mild chilli powder
- 1 tsp ground coriander
- ½ tsp cumin seeds
- 400g can chopped tomatoes
- 196g can sweetcorn in water
- 1 tsp vegetable bouillon powder
- 1 avocado, stoned and chopped
- 1/2 lime, zest and juice
- handful coriander, chopped, plus extra to serve

DIRECTIONS

STEP 1

Cook the pasta in salted water for 10-12 mins until al dente. Meanwhile, heat the oil in a medium pan. Add the sliced onion and pepper and fry, stirring frequently for 10 mins until golden. Stir in the garlic and spices, then tip in the tomatoes, half a can of water, the corn and bouillon. Cover and simmer for 15 mins.

STEP 2

Meanwhile, toss the avocado with the lime juice and zest, and the finely chopped onion.

STEP 3

Drain the penne and toss into the sauce with the coriander. Spoon the pasta into bowls, top with the avocado and scatter over the coriander leaves.

CHOCOLATE-ORANGE STEAMED PUDDING WITH CHOCOLATE SAUCE

Prep: 25 mins - Cook: 1 hr and 30 mins - Serves 8

INGREDIENTS

For the chocolate sauce

- 50g cocoa
- 50g butter , plus extra for greasing
- 100g Total Sweet (xylitol, see tip)
- 1 tsp vanilla extract
- 200ml semi-skimmed milk

For the pudding

- 1 small orange
- 100g Total Sweet (xylitol)
- 225g self-raising flour
- 50g cocoa
- 150ml semi-skimmed milk
- 1 tsp vanilla extract
- 2 large eggs

DIRECTIONS

STEP 1

First, make the sauce. Sift the cocoa into a small saucepan, add all the other INGREDIENTS, then warm over a medium-high heat, stirring. Allow to bubble hard for 1 min to make a glossy sauce. Spoon 4 tbsp into the base of a lightly buttered, traditional 1.2 litre pudding basin. Leave the rest to cool, stirring occasionally.

STEP 2

Put a very large pan (deep enough to enclose the whole pudding basin) of water on to boil with a small upturned plate placed in the base of the pan to support the basin.

STEP 3

Zest the orange, then cut the peel and pith away, and cut between the membrane to release the segments. Put all the pudding INGREDIENTS, except the orange segments, in a food processor and blitz until smooth. Add the orange segments and pulse to chop them into the pudding mixture. Spoon the mixture into the pudding basin, smoothing to the edges.

STEP 4

Tear off a sheet of foil and a sheet of baking parchment, both about 30cm long. Butter the baking parchment and use to cover the foil. Fold a 3cm pleat in the middle of the sheets, then place over the pudding, buttered baking parchment-side down. Tie with string under the lip of the basin, making a handle as you go. Trim the excess parchment and foil to about 5cm, then tuck the foil around the parchment to seal. Lower the basin into the pan of water, checking that the water comes tw o-thirds of the way up the sides of the basin, then cover the pan with a lid to trap the steam and simmer for 1 1/2 hours.

STEP 5

Carefully unwrap the pudding – it should now be risen and firm – and turn out of the basin on to a plate. Spoon over some warmed sauce and serve the rest separately with slices of the pudding.

CINNAMON APPLE PECAN PUDDING

Prep: 10 mins - Cook: 45 mins - Serves 6

INGREDIENTS

- 85g softened butter
- 85g xylitol (we used Total Sweet)
- 125g self-raising flour
- 25g oats
- 1 tsp ground cinnamon
- 1 heaped tsp baking powder
- 2 large eggs

- 3 tbsp milk
- 1 Bramley apple (about 280g), peeled, cored, a quarter grated, the rest diced
- 25g pecans , roughly chopped or broken
- Greek yogurt or cream, to serve

DIRECTIONS

STEP 1

Heat oven to 180C/160C fan/gas 4 and lightly grease a 1-litre (20 x 16cm) pie or oven dish. Tip the butter and xylitol into a bowl with the flour, oats, cinnamon and baking powder. Break in the eggs, add the milk, then beat with an electric hand whisk until evenly mixed and smooth. Stir in all the apple, then scrape into the dish, level the top and scatter with the pecans.

STEP 2

Bake for 35-45 mins until risen and golden and a skewer inserted into the centre comes out clean. Serve with Greek yogurt or cream.

SLOW-COOKER CHICKEN CURRY

Prep: 10 mins - Cook: 6 hrs Plus overnight chilling - Serves 2

INGREDIENTS

- 1 large onion, roughly chopped
- 3 tbsp mild curry paste
- 400g can chopped tomatoes
- 2 tsp vegetable bouillon powder
- 1 tbsp finely chopped ginger
- 1 yellow pepper, deseeded and chopped
- 2 skinless chicken legs, fat removed
- 30g pack fresh coriander, leaves chopped
- cooked brown rice, to serve

DIRECTIONS

STEP 1

Put 1 roughly chopped large onion, 3 tbsp mild curry paste, a 400g can chopped tomatoes, 2 tsp vegetable bouillon powder, 1 tbsp finely chopped ginger and 1 chopped yellow pepper into the slow cooker pot with a third of a can of water and stir well.

STEP 2

Add 2 skinless chicken legs, fat removed, and push them under all the other INGREDIENTS so that they are completely submerged. Cover with the lid and chill in the fridge overnight.

STEP 3

The next day, cook on Low for 6 hrs until the chicken and vegetables are really tender.

STEP 4

Stir in the the chopped leaves of 30g coriander just before serving over brown rice.

SPICED LENTIL & BUTTERNUT SQUASH SOUP

Prep: 10 mins - Cook: 40 mins - Serves 4-6

INGREDIENTS

- 2 tbsp olive oil
- 2 onions, finely chopped
- 2 garlic cloves, crushed
- ¼ tsp hot chilli powder
- 1 tbsp ras el hanout
- 1 butternut squash, peeled and cut into 2cm pieces
- 100g red lentils
- 1l hot vegetable stock
- 1 small bunch coriander, leaves chopped, plus extra to serve
- dukkah (see tip) and natural yogurt, to serve

DIRECTIONS

STEP 1

Heat the oil in a large flameproof casserole dish or saucepan over a medium-high heat. Fry the onions with a pinch of salt for 7 mins, or until softened and just caramelised. Add the garlic, chilli and ras el hanout, and cook for 1 min more.

STEP 2

Stir in the squash and lentils. Pour over the stock and season to taste. Bring to the boil, then reduce the heat to a simmer and cook, covered, for 25 mins or until the squash is soft. Blitz the soup with a stick

blender until smooth, then season to taste. To freeze, leave to cool completely and transfer to large
freezerproof bags.

STEP 3

Stir in the coriander leaves and ladle the soup into bowls. Serve topped with the dukkah, yogurt and extra
coriander leaves.

LOW-FAT SPANISH OMELETTE

Prep: 10 mins - Cook: 15 mins - Serves 1

INGREDIENTS

- 180g sweet potato , peeled and cut into 2cm chunks
- 5ml olive oil
- 55g onion , sliced
- 140g red pepper , diced
- 1 garlic clove , grated
- 5 slices turkey bacon , sliced
- 1 rosemary sprig (optional)
- 5 eggs (1 whole egg and 4 egg whites)
- 2 handfuls green salad leaves
- 150g 0% fat Greek yogurt

DIRECTIONS

STEP 1

Heat oven to 180C/160C fan/gas 4. Heat the sweet potato chunks in the microwave for 3 mins, leave to rest
for 2 mins, then heat again for a further 2 mins, by which time they should be cooked through and soft.

STEP 2

Meanwhile, heat the oil in a nonstick ovenproof frying pan over a medium-high heat. Add the onion,
pepper, turkey, garlic and rosemary (if using), and cook for 2-3 mins. When the potatoes are ready, add
them to the pan as well.

STEP 3

Beat the egg and egg whites together, then pour into the frying pan. Use a spatula to move the eggs around,
scraping it up from the base, for 1-2 mins or until there is a good proportion of cooked egg in the pan and

the ingredients are well mixed. Put the pan in the oven and heat until the egg is cooked through. Slide the omelette from the pan and enjoy with a side salad and a good dollop of yogurt.

LOW-FAT TURKEY BOLOGNESE

Prep: 10 mins Cook: 45 mins

Serves 4 - 6

INGREDIENTS

- 400g lean turkey mince (choose breast instead of thigh mince if you can, as it has less fat)
- 2 tsp vegetable oil
- 1 large onion, chopped
- 1 large carrot, chopped
- 3 celery sticks, chopped
- 250g pack brown mushroom, finely chopped
- pinch of sugar
- 1 tbsp tomato purée
- 2 x 400g cans chopped tomato with garlic & herbs
- 400ml chicken stock, made from 1 low-sodium stock cube
- cooked wholemeal pasta and fresh basil leaves (optional), to serve

DIRECTIONS

STEP 1

Heat a large non-stick frying pan and dry-fry the turkey mince until browned. Tip onto a plate and set aside.

STEP 2

Add the oil and gently cook the onion, carrot and celery until softened, about 10 mins (add a splash of water if it starts to stick). Add the mushrooms and cook for a few mins, then add the sugar and tomato purée, and cook for 1 min more, stirring to stop it from sticking.

STEP 3

Add the tomatoes, turkey and stock with some seasoning. Simmer for at least 20 mins (or longer) until thickened. Serve with the pasta and fresh basil, if you have it.

PRAWN TIKKA MASALA

INGREDIENTS

- 1 large onion , roughly chopped
- 1 thumb-sized piece ginger , peeled and grated
- 2 large garlic cloves
- 1 tbsp rapeseed oil
- 2-3 tbsp tikka curry paste
- 400g can chopped tomatoes
- 2 tbsp tomato purée
- ½ tbsp light brown soft sugar
- 3 cardamom pods , bashed
- 200g brown basmati rice
- 3 tbsp ground almonds
- 300g raw king prawns
- 1 tbsp double cream
- ½ bunch of coriander , roughly chopped
- naan breads , warmed, to serve (optional)

DIRECTIONS

STEP 1

Put the onion, ginger and garlic in a food processor and blitz to a smooth paste. Heat the oil in a large flameproof casserole dish or pan over a medium heat. Add the onion paste and fry for 8 mins or until lightly golden. Stir in the curry paste and fry for 1 min more. Add the tomatoes, tomato purée, sugar and cardamom pods. Bring to a simmer and cook, covered, for another 10 mins.

STEP 2

Cook the rice following pack instructions.

STEP 3

Scoop the cardamom out of the curry sauce and discard, then blitz with a hand blender, or in a clean food processor. Return to the pan, add the almonds and prawns, and cook for 5 mins. Season to taste and stir through the cream and coriander. Serve with the rice and naan breads, if you like.

CHILLI PRAWN LINGUINE

Prep: 5 mins - Cook: 20 mins - 25 mins - Serves 6

INGREDIENTS

- 280g linguine pasta
- 200g sugar snap peas, trimmed
- 2 tbsp olive oil
- 2 large garlic cloves, finely chopped
- 1 large red chilli, deseeded and finely chopped
- 24 raw king prawns, peeled
- 12 cherry tomatoes, halved
- a handful of fresh basil leaves
- mixed salad leaves and crusty white bread, to serve

For the lime dressing

- 2 tbsp virtually fat-free fromage frais
- grated zest and juice of 2 limes
- 2 tsp golden caster sugar

DIRECTIONS

STEP 1

To make the dressing, mix 2 tbsp virtually fat-free fromage frais, the grated zest and juice of 2 limes and 2 tsp golden caster sugar in a small bowl and season with salt and pepper. Set aside.

STEP 2

Cook 280g linguine pasta according to the packet instructions. Add 200g trimmed sugar snap peas for the last minute or so of cooking time.

STEP 3

Meanwhile, heat 2 tbsp olive oil in a wok or big frying pan, toss in 2 finely chopped large garlic cloves and 1 deseeded and finely chopped large red chilli and cook over a fairly gentle heat for about 30 seconds without letting the garlic brown.

STEP 4

Tip in 24 peeled raw king prawns and cook over a high heat, stirring frequently, for about 3 minutes until they turn pink.

STEP 5

Add 12 halved cherry tomatoes and cook, stirring occasionally, for 3 minutes until they just start to soften.

STEP 6

Drain the linguine pasta and sugar snap peas well, then toss into the prawn mixture.

STEP 7

Tear in a handful of basil leaves, stir, and season with salt and pepper.

STEP 8

Serve with mixed salad leaves drizzled with the lime dressing, and warm crusty white bread.

PESTO & GOAT'S CHEESE RISOTTO

Prep: 2 mins - Cook: 30 mins - Serves 2

INGREDIENTS

- olive oil , for frying
- 200g risotto rice
- 700ml chicken stock or vegetable stock
- 1 tub fresh pesto
- 100g soft goat's cheese

DIRECTIONS

STEP 1

Pour a glug of olive oil into a large saucepan. Tip in the rice and fry for 1 min. Add half the stock and cook until absorbed. Add the remaining stock, a ladle at a time, and cook until the rice is al dente, stirring continually, for 20-25 mins.

STEP 2

Stir through the pesto and half the goat's cheese. Serve topped with the remaining cheese.

TAGLIATA & BORLOTTI BEANS

Prep: 15 mins - Cook: 5 mins - Serves 2

INGREDIENTS

- small bunch parsley
- ½ small bunch basil

- 1 small garlic clove
- 3 tbsp olive oil , plus a drizzle
- 1 tbsp red wine vinegar
- 250g rump steak , about 2cm thick
- 400g can borlotti beans , drained and rinsed
- 50g rocket
- 80g cherry tomatoes , halved
- 25g parmesan , shaved (optional)

DIRECTIONS

STEP 1

Put the parsley, basil, garlic, olive oil and 1 tbsp water in the small bowl of a food processor and whizz until the herbs are finely chopped. Transfer to a bowl, stir through the vinegar and season to taste.

STEP 2

Season the steak generously. Heat a griddle pan or non-stick frying pan over a high heat. Drizzle a little extra oil over the steak and fry for 5 mins, turning every minute. Put on a plate, cover and leave for about 5 mins to rest.

STEP 3

Toss the beans, rocket and cherry tomatoes in the herb mixture. Slice the steak into strips. Divide the salad between two plates, top with the steak and scatter over the shaved parmesan, if you like.

VEGGIE YAKI UDON

Prep: 10 mins - Cook: 15 mins - Serves 2

INGREDIENTS

- 1½ tbsp sesame oil
- 1 red onion , cut into thin wedges
- 160g mangetout
- 70g baby corn , halved
- 2 baby pak choi , quartered
- 3 spring onions , sliced
- 1 large garlic clove , crushed
- ½ tbsp mild curry powder
- 4 tsp low-salt soy sauce
- 300g ready-to-cook udon noodles

- 1 tbsp pickled sushi ginger , chopped, plus 2 tbsp of the brine

DIRECTIONS

STEP 1

Heat the oil in a non-stick frying pan or wok over a high heat. Add the onion and fry for 5 mins. Stir in the mangetout, corn, pak choi and spring onions and cook for 5 mins more. Add the garlic, curry powder and soy sauce, and cook for another minute.

STEP 2

Add the udon noodles along with the ginger and reserved brine, and stir in 2-3 tbsp hot water until the noodles are heated through. Divide between bowls and serve.

BOMBAY POTATO FRITTATA

Prep: 15 mins - Cook: 35 mins - Serves 2

INGREDIENTS

- 4 new potatoes , sliced into 5mm rounds
- 100g baby spinach , chopped
- 1 tbsp rapeseed oil
- 1 onion , halved and sliced
- 1 large garlic clove , finely grated
- ½ tsp ground coriander
- ½ tsp ground cumin
- ¼ tsp black mustard seeds
- ¼ tsp turmeric
- 3 tomatoes , roughly chopped
- 2 large eggs
- ½ green chilli , deseeded and finely chopped
- 1 small bunch of coriander , finely chopped
- 1 tbsp mango chutney
- 3 tbsp fat-free Greek yogurt

DIRECTIONS

STEP 1

Cook the potatoes in a pan of boiling water for 6 mins, or until tender. Drain and leave to steam-dry. Meanwhile, put the spinach in a heatproof bowl with 1 tbsp water. Cover and microwave for 3 mins on high, or until wilted.

STEP 2

Heat the rapeseed oil in a medium non-stick frying pan. Add the onion and cook over a medium heat for 10 mins until golden and sticky. Stir in the garlic, ground coriander, ground cumin, mustard seeds and turmeric, and cook for 1 min more. Add the tomatoes and wilted spinach and cook for another 3 mins, then add the potatoes.

STEP 3

Heat the grill to medium. Lightly beat the eggs with the chilli and most of the fresh coriander and pour over the potato mixture. Grill for 4-5 mins, or until golden and just set, with a very slight wobble in the middle.

STEP 4

Leave to cool, then slice into wedges. Mix the mango chutney, yogurt and remaining fresh coriander together. Serve with the frittata wedges.

EASY SLOW COOKER CHICKEN CASSEROLE

Prep: 10 mins - Cook: 4 hrs - 8 hrs - Serves 4

INGREDIENTS

- 1 leek, roughly chopped
- 1 carrot, roughly chopped
- 1 onion, roughly chopped
- 350g new potatoes, roughly chopped
- 6 skinless, boneless chicken thighs, chopped
- 500ml chicken stock
- 4 tbsp vegetable gravy granules

DIRECTIONS

STEP 1

Put the veg and chicken in a slow cooker. Pour the stock over and around the chicken thighs, then mix in the gravy granules to thicken it up (the sauce will be quite thick – use less gravy if you prefer a runnier casserole).

STEP 2

Switch the slow cooker to low and leave to cook for at least 4 hrs, or up to 8 hrs – try putting it on before you go to work, so that it's ready when you get home. Season well, then serve.

SLOW-COOKER VEGETABLE LASAGNE

Prep: 30 mins - Cook: 2 hrs and 30 mins - 3 hrs - Serves 4

INGREDIENTS

- 1 tbsp rapeseed oil
- 2 onions, sliced
- 2 large garlic cloves, chopped
- 2 large courgettes, diced (400g)
- 1 red and 1 yellow pepper, deseeded and roughly sliced
- 400g can chopped tomatoes
- 2 tbsp tomato purée
- 2 tsp vegetable bouillon
- 15g fresh basil, chopped plus a few leaves
- 1 large aubergine, sliced across length or width for maximum surface area
- 6 wholewheat lasagne sheets (105g)
- 125g vegetarian buffalo mozzarella, chopped

DIRECTIONS

STEP 1

Heat 1 tbsp rapeseed oil in a large non-stick pan and fry 2 sliced onions and 2 chopped large garlic cloves for 5 mins, stirring frequently until softened.

STEP 2

Tip in 2 diced large courgettes, 1 red and 1 yellow pepper, both roughly sliced, and 400g chopped tomatoes with 2 tbsp tomato purée, 2 tsp vegetable bouillon and 15g chopped basil.

STEP 3

Stir well, cover and cook for 5 mins. Don't be tempted to add more liquid as plenty of moisture will come from the vegetables once they start cooking.

STEP 4

Slice 1 large aubergine. Lay half the slices of aubergine in the base of the slow cooker and top with 3 sheets of lasagne.

STEP 5

Add a third of the ratatouille mixture, then the remaining aubergine slices, 3 more lasagne sheets, then the remaining ratatouille mixture.

STEP 6

Cover and cook on High for 2½ - 3 hours until the pasta and vegetables are tender. Turn off the machine.

STEP 7

Scatter 125g vegetarian buffalo mozzarella over the vegetables then cover and leave for 10 mins to settle and melt the cheese.

STEP 8

Scatter with extra basil and serve with a handful of rocket.

SPICED HALLOUMI & PINEAPPLE BURGER WITH ZINGY SLAW

Prep: 20 mins - Cook: 5 mins - Serves 2

INGREDIENTS

- ½ red cabbage, grated
- 2 carrots, grated
- 100g radishes, sliced
- 1 small pack coriander, chopped
- 2 limes, juiced
- 1 tbsp cold-pressed rapeseed oil
- big pinch of chilli flakes
- 1 tbsp chipotle paste
- 60g halloumi, cut into 4 slices
- 2 small slices of fresh pineapple
- 1 Little Gem lettuce, divided into 4 lettuce cups, or 2 small seeded burger buns, cut in half, to serve (optional)

DIRECTIONS

STEP 1

Heat the barbecue. Put the cabbage, carrot, radish and coriander in a bowl. Pour over the lime juice, add ½ tbsp oil and the chilli flakes, then season with salt and pepper. Give everything a good mix with your hands. This can be done a few hours before and kept in the fridge.

STEP 2

Mix the remaining oil with the chipotle paste then coat the halloumi slices in the mixture. Put the halloumi slices on a sheet of foil and put on the barbecue with the pineapple (or use a searing hot griddle pan if cooking inside). Cook for 2 mins on each side until the cheese is golden, and the pineapple is beginning to caramelise. Brush the buns with the remaining chipotle oil, then put your burger buns, if using, cut-side down, on the barbecue for the last 30 seconds of cooking to toast.

STEP 3

Assemble your burgers with the lettuce or buns. Start with a handful of the slaw, then add halloumi and pineapple. Serve with the remaining slaw.

LOW SUGAR CHOCOLATE SANDWICH CAKE

Prep: 35 mins - Cook: 25 mins - 30 mins - Cuts into 12

INGREDIENTS

For the cake

- 150ml rapeseed oil , plus extra for greasing
- 250g cooked beetroot
- 50g cocoa
- 140g plain wholewheat flour
- 100g plain white flour
- 50g ground almonds
- 200g xylitol , such as Total Sweet
- 2 tsp baking powder
- 1 tsp bicarbonate of soda
- 2 large eggs
- 2 tsp vanilla extract
- 50ml skimmed milk

For the chocolate cream

- 150ml pot natural bio-yogurt
- 2 tbsp cocoa
- 100g xylitol such as Total Sweet
- 150ml pot double cream

DIRECTIONS

STEP 1

Heat oven to 160C/140C/gas 3 and grease then line the base of two x 20cm sandwich tins with baking parchment. To start making the chocolate cream stir the yogurt with the cocoa and xylitol until completely blended then set aside while you make the cake. This helps to dissolve the xylitol granules.

STEP 2

To make the cake, first blitz the beetroot in a food processor until it resembles a thick puree. Tip in the cocoa, flours, ground almonds, xylitol, baking powder and soda and pulse briefly to mix the INGREDIENTS together.

STEP 3

Now add the eggs, the 150ml rapeseed oil, vanilla extract and milk, and blitz again to make a smooth liquid batter.

STEP 4

Divide the mixture evenly between the tins working quickly, as the baking powder activates once in contact with the liquid INGREDIENTS, then bake for 25-30 mins until a skewer poked into the middle of the cake comes out clean. Cool for few mins then remove from the tins and finish cooling on a wire rack. Once cold, carefully strip off the lining paper.

STEP 5

To finish the chocolate cream, whip the double cream until it holds its shape. Stir the cocoa mixture then fold in all but 2 tsp. Spread a third on top of one of the cold sponge cakes, top with the remaining sponge and spread with the rest of the chocolate cream to create a swirly finish. Dot over the reserved cocoa mixture and gently feather in with the end of a teaspoon. The cake will keep in the fridge for a couple of days, but return to room temperature before eating for the best taste and texture.

SUPER-QUICK SESAME RAMEN

Prep: 5 mins - Cook: 10 mins - Serves 1

INGREDIENTS

- 80g pack instant noodles (look for an Asian brand with a flavour like sesame)
- 2 spring onions , finely chopped
- ½ head pak choi
- 1 egg
- 1 tsp sesame seeds
- chilli sauce , to serve

DIRECTIONS

STEP 1

Cook the noodles with the sachet of flavouring provided (or use stock instead of the sachet, if you have it). Add the spring onions and pak choi for the final min.

STEP 2

Meanwhile, simmer the egg for 6 mins from boiling, run it under cold water to stop it cooking, then peel it. Toast the sesame seeds in a frying pan.

STEP 3

Tip the noodles and greens into a deep bowl, halve the boiled egg and place on top. Sprinkle with sesame seeds, then drizzle with the sauce or sesame oil provided with the noodles, and chilli sauce, if using.

SMOKY SPICED VEGGIE RICE

Prep: 15 mins - Cook: 1 hr - Serves 6

INGREDIENTS

- 25g cashews
- 4 tbsp olive oil
- 1 corn cob
- 250g rainbow baby carrots , halved lengthways
- 2 red onions , finely chopped
- 2 celery sticks , finely chopped
- 2 large red peppers , finely sliced
- 3 garlic cloves , crushed
- 2 tbsp Cajun seasoning
- 1½ tbsp smoked paprika
- 1 tsp chipotle paste
- 2 tbsp tomato purée
- 200g heirloom cherry tomatoes , halved
- 400g can kidney beans , drained and rinsed
- 400g can cherry tomatoes
- 300g long-grain rice , washed
- 400ml vegetable or vegan stock
- 1 tbsp red wine vinegar (vegan varieties are readily available)
- 2 tbsp caster sugar
- 2 spring onions , finely sliced

DIRECTIONS

STEP 1

Dry-fry the cashews in a large saucepan or casserole dish over a medium heat until golden brown. Remove from the heat, leave to cool, then roughly chop. Heat 1 tbsp oil in the same pan over a high heat, then fry the corn on each side for 20 seconds to char. Remove from the pan, set aside, then tip in the carrots and fry for 5 mins. Remove from the pan and set aside.

STEP 2

Heat the rest of the oil in the same pan over a medium heat and fry the onions and celery for 10 mins until soft and slightly coloured. Tip in the peppers and garlic, then fry for another 5 mins before adding the Cajun seasoning, smoked paprika, chipotle paste and tomato purée. Fry for 1 min until the spices are fragrant, then add the cherry tomatoes and fry for another 2 mins.

STEP 3

Stir in the kidney beans, canned tomatoes, rice, stock, vinegar and sugar, then stir until everything is combined. Bring to the boil, then cover with a lid and simmer with a lid on for 35-40 mins on a medium-low heat, stirring halfway through, until the rice is cooked and liquid absorbed.

STEP 4

Slice the corn off the cob and mix it through the rice along with the carrots. Season and garnish with the spring onions and cashews.

SPICED CHICKEN, SPINACH & SWEET POTATO STEW

Prep: 15 mins - Cook: 40 mins - Serves 4

INGREDIENTS

- 3 sweet potatoes, cut into chunks
- 190g bag spinach
- 1 tbsp sunflower oil
- 8 chicken thighs, skinless and boneless
- 500ml chicken stock

For the spice paste

- 2 onions, chopped
- 1 red chilli, chopped
- 1 tsp paprika
- thumb-sized piece ginger, grated
- 400g can tomatoes
- 2 preserved lemons, deseeded and chopped

To serve

- pumpkin seeds, toasted
- 2-3 preserved lemons, deseeded and chopped
- 4 naan bread, warmed

DIRECTIONS

STEP 1

Put the sweet potato in a large, deep saucepan over a high heat. Cover with boiling water and boil for 10 mins. Meanwhile, put all the paste INGREDIENTS in a food processor and blend until very finely chopped. Set aside until needed.

STEP 2

Put the spinach in a large colander in the sink and pour the sweet potatoes and their cooking water over it to drain the potatoes and wilt the spinach at the same time. Leave to steam-dry.

STEP 3

Return the saucepan to the heat (no need to wash it first), then add the oil, followed by the spice paste. Fry the paste for about 5 mins until thickened, then add the chicken. Fry for 8-10 mins until the chicken starts to colour. Pour over the stock, bring to the boil and leave to simmer for 10 mins, stirring occasionally.

STEP 4

Check the chicken is cooked by cutting into one of the thighs and making sure it's white throughout with no signs of pink. Season with black pepper, then add the sweet potato. Leave to simmer for a further 5 mins. Meanwhile, roughly chop the spinach and add to the stew. At this point you can leave the stew to cool and freeze for up to 3 months, if you like.

STEP 5

Scatter over the pumpkin seeds and preserved lemons, and serve with warm naan bread on the side.

PRAWN JAMBALAYA

Prep: 10 mins - Cook: 35 mins - Serves 2

INGREDIENTS

- 1 tbsp rapeseed oil
- 1 onion , chopped
- 3 celery sticks , sliced
- 100g wholegrain basmati rice

- 1 tsp mild chilli powder
- 1 tbsp ground coriander
- ½ tsp fennel seeds
- 400g can chopped tomatoes
- 1 tsp vegetable bouillon powder
- 1 yellow pepper , roughly chopped
- 2 garlic cloves , chopped
- 1 tbsp fresh thyme leaves
- 150g pack small prawns , thawed if frozen
- 3 tbsp chopped parsley

DIRECTIONS

STEP 1

Heat the oil in a large, deep frying pan. Add the onion and celery, and fry for 5 mins to soften. Add the rice and spices, and pour in the tomatoes with just under 1 can of water. Stir in the bouillon powder, pepper, garlic and thyme.

STEP 2

Cover the pan with a lid and simmer for 30 mins until the rice is tender and almost all the liquid has been absorbed. Stir in the prawns and parsley, cook briefly to heat through, then serve.

MEDITERRANEAN TURKEY-STUFFED PEPPERS

Prep: 20 mins - Cook: 30 mins - Serves 2

INGREDIENTS

- 2 red peppers (about 220g)
- 1 ½ tbsp olive oil, plus an extra drizzle
- 240g lean turkey breast mince (under 8% fat)
- ½ small onion, chopped
- 1 garlic clove, grated
- 1 tsp ground cumin
- 3-4 mushrooms, sliced
- 400g can chopped tomatoes
- 1 tbsp tomato purée
- 1 chicken stock cube
- handful fresh oregano leaves

- 60g mozzarella, grated
- 150g green vegetables (spinach, kale, broccoli, mangetout or green beans), to serve

DIRECTIONS

STEP 1

Heat oven to 190C/170C fan/gas 5. Halve the peppers lengthways, then remove the seeds and core but keep the stalks on. Rub the peppers with a drizzle of olive oil and season well. Put on a baking tray and roast for 15 mins.

STEP 2

Meanwhile, heat 1 tbsp olive oil in a large pan over a medium heat. Fry the mince for 2-3 mins, stirring to break up the chunks, then tip onto a plate.

STEP 3

Wipe out your pan, then heat the rest of the oil over a medium-high heat. Add the onion and garlic, stir-fry for 2-3 mins, then add the cumin and mushrooms and cook for 2-3 mins more.

STEP 4

Tip the mince back into the pan and add the chopped tomatoes and tomato purée. Crumble in the stock cube and cook for 3-4 mins, then add the oregano and season. Remove the peppers from the oven and fill them with as much of the mince as you can. (Don't worry if some spills out it – it will go satisfyingly crisp in the oven.) Top with the cheese and return to the oven for 10-15 mins until the cheese starts to turn golden.

STEP 5

Carefully slide the peppers onto a plate and serve alongside a pile of your favourite greens blanched, boiled or steamed.

MANGO SORBET

Prep: 15 mins plus freezing - Serves 8

INGREDIENTS

- 3 large, ripe mangoes
- 200g caster sugar
- 1 lime , juiced

DIRECTIONS

STEP 1

Peel the mangoes with a vegetable peeler, cut as much of the flesh away from the stone as you can, put it in a food processor or blender.

STEP 2

Add the sugar, lime juice and 200ml water. Blend for a few minutes, until the mango is very smooth and the sugar has dissolved – rub a little of the mixture between your fingers, if it still feels gritty, blend for a little longer. Pour into a container and put in the freezer for a few hours.

STEP 3

Scrape the sorbet back into the blender (if it's very solid, leave at room temperature for 5-10 mins first). Whizz until you have a slushy mixture, then pour back into the tin and freeze for another hour or so.

STEP 4

Repeat step 3. Freeze until solid (another hour or two). Will keep covered in the freezer for three months.

CREAMY CHICKEN & ASPARAGUS BRAISE

Prep: 10 mins - Cook: 20 mins - 25 mins - Serves 2

INGREDIENTS

- 1 tbsp rapeseed oil
- 2 skinless chicken breasts (about 150g each)
- 10 medium asparagus spears , each cut into 3
- 1 large or 2 small leeks , well washed and thickly sliced
- 3 celery sticks , sliced
- 200ml reduced-salt vegetable bouillon
- 140g frozen peas
- 1 egg yolk
- 4 tbsp natural bio yogurt
- 1 garlic clove , finely grated
- ⅓ small pack fresh tarragon , chopped
- new potatoes , to serve (optional)

DIRECTIONS

STEP 1

Heat the oil in a large non-stick frying pan and fry the chicken for 5 mins, turning to brown both sides.

STEP 2

Add the asparagus (reserve the tips), leeks and celery, pour in the bouillon and simmer for 10 mins. Add the asparagus tips and peas, and cook for 5 mins more.

STEP 3

Meanwhile, stir the egg yolk with the yogurt and garlic. Stir the yogurt mixture into the vegetables and add the tarragon. Divide between two warm plates, then place the chicken on top of the vegetables. Serve with new potatoes, if you like.

LOW-FAT CHICKEN BIRYANI

Prep: 25 mins - Cook: 1 hr and 35 mins Plus marinating - Serves 5

INGREDIENTS

- 3 garlic cloves , finely grated
- 2 tsp finely grated ginger
- ¼ tsp ground cinnamon
- 1 tsp turmeric
- 5 tbsp natural yogurt
- 600g boneless, skinless chicken breast , cut into 4-5cm pieces
- 2 tbsp semi-skimmed milk
- good pinch saffron
- 4 medium onions
- 4 tbsp rapeseed oil
- ½ tsp hot chilli powder
- 1 cinnamon stick , broken in half
- 5 green cardamom pods , lightly bashed to split
- 3 cloves
- 1 tsp cumin seed
- 280g basmati rice
- 700ml chicken stock
- 1 tsp garam masala
- handful chopped coriander leaves

DIRECTIONS

STEP 1

In a mixing bowl, stir together the garlic, ginger, cinnamon, turmeric and yogurt with some pepper and ¼ tsp salt. Tip in the chicken pieces and stir to coat (see step 1, above). Cover and marinate in the fridge for about 1 hr or longer if you have time. Warm the milk to tepid, stir in the saffron and set aside.

STEP 2

Heat oven to 200C/180C fan/gas 6. Slice each onion in half lengthways, reserve half and cut the other half into thin slices. Pour 1½ tbsp of the oil onto a baking tray, scatter over the sliced onion, toss to coat, then spread out in a thin, even layer (step 2). Roast for 40-45 mins, stirring halfway, until golden.

STEP 3

When the chicken has marinated, thinly slice the reserved onion. Heat 1 tbsp oil in a large sauté or frying pan. Fry the onion for 4-5 mins until golden. Stir in the chicken, a spoonful at a time, frying until it is no longer opaque, before adding the next spoonful (this helps to prevent the yogurt from curdling). Once the last of the chicken has been added, stir-fry for a further 5 mins until everything looks juicy. Scrape any sticky bits off the bottom of the pan, stir in the chilli powder, then pour in 100ml water, cover and simmer on a low heat for 15 mins. Remove and set aside.

STEP 4

Cook the rice while the chicken simmers. Heat another 1 tbsp oil in a large sauté pan, then drop in the cinnamon stick, cardamom, cloves and cumin seeds. Fry briefly until their aroma is released. Tip in the rice (step 3) and fry for 1 min, stirring constantly. Stir in the stock and bring to the boil. Lower the heat and simmer, covered, for about 8 mins or until all the stock has been absorbed. Remove from the heat and leave with the lid on for a few mins, so the rice can fluff up. Stir the garam masala into the remaining 1½ tsp oil and set aside. When the onions are roasted, remove and reduce oven to 180C/160C fan/gas 4.

STEP 5

Spoon half the chicken and its juices into an ovenproof dish, about 25 x 18 x 6cm, then scatter over a third of the roasted onions. Remove the whole spices from the rice, then layer half of the rice over the chicken and onions. Drizzle over the spiced oil. Spoon over the rest of the chicken and a third more onions. Top with the remaining rice (step 4) and drizzle over the saffron-infused milk. Scatter over the rest of the onions, cover tightly with foil and heat through in the oven for about 25 mins. Serve scattered with the mint and coriander.

SLOW COOKER SHEPHERD'S PIE

Prep: 1 hr - Cook: 5 hrs - Serves 4

INGREDIENTS

- 1 tbsp olive oil
- 1 onion, finely chopped
- 3-4 thyme sprigs
- 2 carrots, finely diced
- 250g lean (10%) mince lamb or beef

- 1 tbsp plain flour
- 1 tbsp tomato purée
- 400g can lentils, or white beans
- 1 tsp Worcestershire sauce

For the topping

- 650g potatoes, peeled and cut into chunks
- 250g sweet potatoes, peeled and cut into chunks
- 2 tbsp half-fat crème fraîche

DIRECTIONS

STEP 1

Heat the slow cooker if necessary. Heat the oil in a large frying pan. Tip the onions and thyme sprigs and fry for 2-3 mins. Then add the carrots and fry together, stirring occasionally until the vegetables start to brown. Stir in the mince and fry for 1-2 mins until no longer pink. Stir in the flour then cook for another 1-2 mins. Stir in the tomato purée and lentils and season with pepper and the Worcestershire sauce, adding a splash of water if you think the mixture is too dry. Scrape everything into the slow cooker.

STEP 2

Meanwhile cook both lots of potatoes in simmering water for 12-13 minutes or until they are cooked through. Drain well and then mash with the crème fraîche. Spoon this on top of the mince mixture and cook on Low for 5 hours - the mixture should be bubbling at the sides when it is ready. Crisp up the potato topping under the grill if you like.

CHUNKY VEGETABLE & BROWN RICE SOUP

Prep: 18 mins - Cook: 50 mins - Serves 4

INGREDIENTS

- 2 tbsp cold-pressed rapeseed oil
- 1 medium onion , halved and sliced
- 2 garlic cloves , finely sliced
- 2 celery sticks , trimmed and thinly sliced
- 2medium carrots , cut into chunks
- 2 medium parsnips , cut into chunks
- 1 tbsp finely chopped thyme leaves
- 100g wholegrain rice

- 2medium leeks , sliced
- ½ small pack parsley , to garnish

DIRECTIONS

STEP 1

Heat the oil in a large non-stick pan and add the onion, garlic, celery, carrots, parsnips and thyme. Cover with a lid and cook gently for 15 mins, stirring occasionally, until the onions are softened and beginning to colour. Add the rice and pour in 1.2 litres cold water. Bring to the boil, then reduce the heat to a simmer and cook, uncovered, for 15 mins, stirring occasionally.

STEP 2

Season the soup with plenty of ground black pepper and salt to taste, then stir in the leeks. Return to a gentle simmer and cook for a further 5 mins or until the leeks have softened. Adjust the seasoning to taste and blitz half the soup with a stick blender, leaving the other half chunky, if you like. Top with the parsley and serve in deep bowls.

CURRIED SPINACH, EGGS & CHICKPEAS

Prep: 15 mins - Cook: 35 mins - Serves 2

INGREDIENTS

- 1 tbsp rapeseed oil
- 1 onion , thinly sliced
- 1 garlic clove , crushed
- 3cm piece ginger , peeled and grated
- 1 tsp ground turmeric
- 1 tsp ground coriander
- 1 tsp garam masala
- 1 tbsp ground cumin
- 450g tomatoes , chopped
- 400g can chickpeas , drained
- 1 tsp sugar
- 200g spinach
- 2 large eggs
- 3 tbsp natural yogurt
- 1 red chilli , finely sliced
- ½ small bunch of coriander , torn

DIRECTIONS

STEP 1

Heat the oil in a large frying pan or flameproof casserole pot over a medium heat, and fry the onion for 10 mins until golden and sticky. Add the garlic, ginger, turmeric, ground coriander, garam masala, cumin and tomatoes, and fry for 2 mins more. Add the chickpeas, 100ml water and the sugar and bring to a simmer. Stir in the spinach, then cover and cook for 20-25 mins. Season to taste.

STEP 2

Cook the eggs in a pan of boiling water for 7 mins, then rinse under cold running water to cool. Drain, peel and halve. Swirl the yogurt into the curry, then top with the eggs, chilli and coriander. Season.

CABBAGE SOUP

Prep: 20 mins - Cook: 50 mins - Serves 6

INGREDIENTS

- 2 tbsp olive oil
- 1 large onion , finely chopped
- 2 celery sticks , finely chopped
- 1 large carrot , finely chopped
- 70g smoked pancetta , diced (optional)
- 1 large Savoy cabbage , shredded
- 2 fat garlic cloves , crushed
- 1 heaped tsp sweet smoked paprika
- 1 tbsp finely chopped rosemary
- 1 x 400g can chopped tomatoes
- 1.7l hot vegetable stock
- 1 x 400g can chickpeas , drained and rinsed
- shaved parmesan (or vegetarian alternative), to serve (optional)
- crusty bread , to serve (optional)

DIRECTIONS

STEP 1

Heat the oil in a casserole pot over a low heat. Add the onion, celery and carrot, along with a generous pinch of salt, and fry gently for 15 mins, or until the veg begins to soften. If you're using pancetta, add it to the pan, turn up the heat and fry for a few mins more until turning golden brown. Tip in the cabbage and fry for 5 mins, then stir through the garlic, paprika and rosemary and cook for 1 min more.

STEP 2

Tip the chopped tomatoes and stock into the pan. Bring to a simmer, then cook, uncovered, for 30 mins, adding the chickpeas for the final 10 mins. Season generously with salt and black pepper.

STEP 3

Ladle the soup into six deep bowls. Serve with the shaved parmesan and crusty bread, if you like.

RED PEPPER, SQUASH & HARISSA SOUP

Prep: 15 mins - Cook: 1 hr - Serves 6

INGREDIENTS

- 1 small butternut squash (about 600-700g), peeled and cut into chunks
- 2 red pepper , roughly chopped
- 2 red onion , roughly chopped
- 3 tbsp rapeseed oil
- 3 garlic cloves in their skins
- 1 tbsp ground coriander
- 2 tsp ground cumin
- 1.2l chicken or vegetable stock
- 2 tbsp harissa paste
- 50ml double cream

DIRECTIONS

STEP 1

Heat oven to 180C/160C fan/gas 4. Put all the veg on a large baking tray and toss together with rapeseed oil, garlic cloves in their skins, ground coriander, ground cumin and some seasoning. Roast for 45 mins, moving the veg around in the tray after 30 mins, until soft and starting to caramelise. Squeeze the garlic cloves out of their skins. Tip everything into a large pan. Add the chicken or vegetable stock, harissa paste and double cream. Bring to a simmer and bubble for a few mins. Blitz the soup in a blender, check the seasoning and add more liquid if you need to. Serve swirled with extra cream and harissa.

LINGUINE WITH AVOCADO, TOMATO & LIME

Prep: 20 mins - Cook: 10 mins - Serves 2

INGREDIENTS

- 115g wholemeal linguine

- 1 lime, zested and juiced
- 1 avocado, stoned, peeled, and chopped
- 2 large ripe tomatoes, chopped
- ½ pack fresh coriander, chopped
- 1 red onion, finely chopped
- 1 red chilli, deseeded and finely chopped (optional)

DIRECTIONS

STEP 1

Cook the pasta according to pack instructions – about 10 mins. Meanwhile, put the lime juice and zest in a medium bowl with the avocado, tomatoes, coriander, onion and chilli, if using, and mix well.

STEP 2

Drain the pasta, toss into the bowl and mix well. Serve straight away while still warm, or cold.

ROASTED ROOTS & SAGE SOUP

Prep: 15 mins - Cook: 45 mins - Serves 2

INGREDIENTS

- 1 parsnip , peeled and chopped
- 2 carrots , peeled and chopped
- 300g turnip , swede or celeriac, chopped
- 4 garlic cloves , skin left on
- 1 tbsp rapeseed oil , plus ½ tsp
- 1 tsp maple syrup
- ¼ small bunch of sage , leaves picked, 4 whole, the rest finely chopped
- 750ml vegetable stock
- grating of nutmeg
- 1½ tbsp fat-free yogurt

DIRECTIONS

STEP 1

Heat the oven to 200C/180C fan/gas 6. Toss the root vegetables and garlic with 1 tbsp oil and season. Tip onto a baking tray and roast for 30 mins until tender. Toss with the maple syrup and the chopped sage, then roast for another 10 mins until golden and glazed. Brush the whole sage leaves with ½ tsp oil and add to the baking tray in the last 3-4 mins to crisp up, then remove and set aside.

STEP 2

Scrape the vegetables into a pan, squeeze the garlic out of the skins, discarding the papery shells, and add with the stock, then blend with a stick blender until very smooth and creamy. Bring to a simmer and season with salt, pepper and nutmeg.

STEP 3

Divide between bowls. Serve with a swirl of yogurt and the crispy sage leaves.

SWEDISH MEATBALLS

Prep: 10 mins - Cook: 25 mins plus cooling and chilling - Serves 4

INGREDIENTS

- 2 tbsp rapeseed oil
- 1 onion , finely chopped
- 1 small garlic clove , finely grated
- 375g lean pork mince
- 1 medium egg yolk
- grating of nutmeg
- 50g fine fresh breadcrumbs
- 300ml hot low-salt beef stock
- ½ tbsp Dijon mustard
- 2 tbsp fat-free natural yogurt
- 400g spring greens , shredded
- lingonberry or cranberry sauce , to serve

DIRECTIONS

STEP 1

Put 1 tbsp rapeseed oil in a frying pan over a medium heat. Add the onion and fry for 10 mins or until soft and translucent. Add the garlic and cook for 1 min. Leave to cool.

STEP 2

Mix the cooled onions, pork mince, egg yolk, a good grating of nutmeg and the breadcrumbs in a bowl with your hands until well combined. Form into 12 balls and chill for 15 mins.

STEP 3

Heat the remaining oil in a frying pan and fry the meatballs for 5 mins over a medium heat, turning often until golden. Pour over the stock and bubble for 8-10 mins or until it has reduced a little. Stir through the mustard and yogurt.

STEP 4

Steam the greens for 5 mins or until tender. Serve the meatballs with the greens and a dollop of the sauce.

SINGAPORE NOODLES WITH PRAWNS

Prep: 10 mins - Cook: 10 mins - Serves 2

INGREDIENTS

- 2 nests thin vermicelli rice noodles
- 1 tbsp light soy sauce
- 1 tbsp oyster sauce
- 2 tsp mild curry powder
- 1 tbsp sesame oil
- 1 garlic clove , chopped
- 1 red chilli , thinly sliced (deseeded if you don't like it too hot)
- thumb-sized piece ginger , grated
- 1 medium onion , sliced
- 1 red pepper or yellow pepper, cut into thin batons
- 4 spring onions , cut in half lengthways then into batons
- 8 raw king prawns
- 1 large egg , beaten
- coriander leaves, to serve

DIRECTIONS

STEP 1

Soak the rice noodles in warm water for 5 mins until softened but still al dente. Drain and set aside.

STEP 2

In a small bowl, mix together the soy, oyster sauce and curry powder.

STEP 3

In a large wok, add half the oil and fry the garlic, chilli and ginger until golden, about 2 mins. Add the remaining oil, onion, pepper, spring onions, prawns and noodles and stir-fry for a few mins. Push everything to one side, add the egg and scramble. Add the soy sauce mixture, toss again for a few more mins, then remove from the heat. Sprinkle over the coriander leaves before serving.

SPICED CARROT & LENTIL SOUP

INGREDIENTS

- 2 tsp cumin seeds
- pinch chilli flakes
- 2 tbsp olive oil
- 600g carrots, washed and coarsely grated (no need to peel)
- 140g split red lentils
- 1l hot vegetable stock (from a cube is fine)
- 125ml milk (to make it dairy-free, see 'try' below)
- plain yogurt and naan bread, to serve

DIRECTIONS

STEP 1

Heat a large saucepan and dry-fry 2 tsp cumin seeds and a pinch of chilli flakes for 1 min, or until they start to jump around the pan and release their aromas.

STEP 2

Scoop out about half with a spoon and set aside. Add 2 tbsp olive oil, 600g coarsely grated carrots, 140g split red lentils, 1l hot vegetable stock and 125ml milk to the pan and bring to the boil.

STEP 3

Simmer for 15 mins until the lentils have swollen and softened.

STEP 4

Whizz the soup with a stick blender or in a food processor until smooth (or leave it chunky if you prefer).

STEP 5

Season to taste and finish with a dollop of plain yogurt and a sprinkling of the reserved toasted spices. Serve with warmed naan breads.

CHANA MASALA WITH POMEGRANATE RAITA

Prep: 10 mins - Cook: 35 mins - Serves 2

INGREDIENTS

- 1 tbsp rapeseed oil

* 2 onions , halved and thinly sliced
* 1 tbsp chopped ginger
* 2 large garlic cloves , finely grated or crushed
* 1 green chilli , halved, deseeded and thinly sliced
* ½ tsp cumin seeds
* ½ tsp mustard seeds
* ½ tsp garam masala
* ½ tsp turmeric
* 1 tsp ground coriander
* 400g can chickpeas , undrained
* 4 small tomatoes (about 160g), cut into wedges
* 2 tsp vegetable bouillon powder
* cooked wholegrain rice , to serve (optional)

For the pomegranate raita

* 150ml plain bio yogurt
* 25g pomegranate seeds
* 2 tbsp finely chopped coriander , plus extra leaves to serve

DIRECTIONS

STEP 1

Heat the oil in a large non-stick pan, then cook the onions, ginger, garlic and chilli for 15-20 mins.

STEP 2

Add the spices, chickpeas, the liquid from the can, ¾ can cold water, the tomatoes and bouillon. Cover and simmer for 10 mins.

STEP 3

Meanwhile, mix the ingredients for the raita in a small bowl, reserving a few coriander leaves. Roughly mash some of the curry to thicken it. Spoon into bowls with rice, if you like. Scatter over the reserved coriander and serve with the raita on the side.

LEEK, PEA & WATERCRESS SOUP

Prep: 10 mins - Cook: 22 mins - Serves 4

INGREDIENTS

* 1 tbsp olive oil , plus a drizzle to serve
* 2 leeks , finely sliced

- 4 small garlic cloves , crushed
- 650-800ml hot veg stock
- 80g watercress
- 400g frozen peas
- 1 small lemon , zested and juiced
- small bunch of parsley , finely chopped
- dairy-free crème fraîche and crusty bread, to serve (optional)

DIRECTIONS

STEP 1

Heat the oil in a large saucepan over a medium heat. Add the leeks and garlic and fry for 7-10 mins or until softened and translucent.

STEP 2

Pour in the hot stock and simmer for 5-10 mins. Stir through the watercress, reserving a few leaves for garnish, then the peas, and cook for 5 mins until wilted. Use a hand blender or processor and whizz until smooth. Stir through the lemon juice and zest, then season to taste. Stir through half the parsley. Ladle into bowls and top with the remaining parsley, reserved watercress and a drizzle of olive oil. Swirl through some crème fraîche, then serve with crusty bread, if you like.

SLOW COOKER LASAGNE

Prep: 1 hr and 15 mins - Cook: 3 hrs - Serves 4

INGREDIENTS

- 2 tsp rapeseed oil
- 2 onions, finely chopped
- 4 celery sticks (about 175g), finely diced
- 4 carrots (320g), finely diced
- 2 garlic cloves, chopped
- 400g lean (5% fat) mince beef
- 400g can chopped tomatoes
- 2 tbsp tomato purée
- 2 tsp vegetable bouillon
- 1 tbsp balsamic vinegar
- 1 tbsp fresh thyme leaves
- 6 wholewheat lasagne sheets (105g)

For the sauce

- 400ml whole milk
- 50g wholemeal flour
- 1 bay leaf
- generous grating of nutmeg
- 15g finely grated parmesan

DIRECTIONS

STEP 1

Heat the slow cooker if necessary. Heat the oil in a large non-stick pan and fry the onions, celery, carrots and garlic for 5-10 mins, stirring frequently until softened and starting to colour. Tip in the meat and break it down with a wooden spoon, stirring until it browns. Pour in the tomatoes with a quarter of a can of water, the tomato purée, bouillon, balsamic vinegar, thyme and plenty of black pepper, return to the boil and cook for 5 mins more.

STEP 2

Spoon half the mince in the slow cooker and top with half the lasagne, breaking it where necessary so it covers as much of the meat layer as possible. Top with the rest of the meat, and then another layer of the lasagne. Cover and cook on Low while you make the sauce.

STEP 3

Tip the milk and flour into a pan with the bay leaf and nutmeg and cook on the hob, whisking continuously until thickened. Carry on cooking for a few mins to cook the flour. Remove the bay leaf and stir in the cheese. Pour onto the pasta and spread out with a spatula, then cover and cook for 3 hours until the meat is cooked and the pasta is tender. Allow to settle for 10 mins before serving with salad.

CAULIFLOWER RICE

Prep: 3 mins - Cook: 7 mins - Serves 4

INGREDIENTS

- 1 medium cauliflower
- good handful coriander, chopped
- cumin seeds, toasted (optional)

DIRECTIONS

STEP 1

Cut the hard core and stalks from the cauliflower and pulse the rest in a food processor to make grains the size of rice. Tip into a heatproof bowl, cover with cling film, then pierce and microwave for 7 mins on High – there is no need to add any water. Stir in the coriander. For spicier rice, add some toasted cumin seeds.

ITALIAN BORLOTTI BEAN, PUMPKIN & FARRO SOUP

Prep: 15 mins - Cook: 35 mins - Serves 6

INGREDIENTS

- 4 tbsp extra virgin olive oil , plus extra to serve
- 1 onion , finely chopped
- 1 celery stick , cut into chunks
- 750g pumpkin or squash, peeled, deseeded and cut into small chunks
- 1 carrot , peeled and cut into chunks
- 3 garlic cloves , chopped
- 3 tbsp tomato purée
- 1.2l chicken stock or vegetable stock
- 75g farro or mixed grains (such as barley or spelt)
- 50-80g parmesan rinds or vegetarian alternative (optional), plus a few shavings to serve
- 400g can borlotti beans , drained
- 2 handfuls baby spinach
- 2 tbsp chopped parsley or 8 whole sage leaves

DIRECTIONS

STEP 1

Heat the oil in a heavy-bottomed saucepan. Add the onion, celery, pumpkin or squash and carrot and cook until the vegetables have some colour. Add a splash of water and some seasoning, then cover the pan and let the vegetables cook over a very low heat for 5 mins.

STEP 2

Add the garlic and cook for another couple of mins, then add the tomato purée, stock, mixed grains, parmesan rinds, if using, and some seasoning. Simmer for about 15 mins (or until the grains are cooked), adding the beans for the final 5 mins. In the last few mins, add the spinach, then taste for seasoning.

STEP 3

If you want to use sage, fry the leaves whole in a little olive oil before adding to the soup. If you prefer to use parsley, you can just add it directly to the soup. Serve with shavings of parmesan and a drizzle of extra virgin olive oil on top of each bowlful. Remove the parmesan rinds and serve.

ASPARAGUS & NEW POTATO FRITTATA

Prep: 10 mins - Cook: 12 mins - Serves 3

INGREDIENTS

- 200g new potatoes, quartered
- 100g asparagus tips
- 1 tbsp olive oil
- 1 onion, finely chopped
- 6 eggs, beaten
- 40g cheddar, grated
- rocket or mixed leaves, to serve

DIRECTIONS

STEP 1

Heat the grill to high. Put the potatoes in a pan of cold salted water and bring to the boil. Once boiling, cook for 4-5 mins until nearly tender, then add the asparagus for a final 1 min. Drain.

STEP 2

Meanwhile, heat the oil in an ovenproof frying pan and add the onion. Cook for about 8 mins until softened.

STEP 3

Mix the eggs with half the cheese in a jug and season well. Pour over the onion in the pan, then scatter over the asparagus and potatoes. Top with the remaining cheese and put under the grill for 5 mins or until golden and cooked through. Cut into wedges and serve from the pan with salad.

MOROCCAN ROAST LAMB WITH ROASTED ROOTS & CORIANDER

Prep: 15 mins - Cook: 55 mins - Serves 4

INGREDIENTS

- ½ leg of lamb , around 800g
- 2 red onions , cut into wedges

- 1 butternut squash , skin left on, cut into wedges
- 1 celeriac , peeled and cut into wedges
- 2½ tbsp cold pressed rapeseed oil
- 2 tbsp ras el hanout
- 8 garlic cloves , skin on
- 1 small bunch coriander
- ½ tsp cumin seeds
- 1 lemon , zested and juiced
- 1/2 green chilli , deseeded

DIRECTIONS

STEP 1

Take the lamb out of the fridge while you chop the onions, squash and celeriac. Heat oven to 200C/180C fan/gas 6. Trim any excess fat off the leg of lamb, then cut a few slashes into the meat. Rub ½ tbsp oil and 1 tbsp ras el hanout over the lamb and season with salt and pepper. Put the onion, celeriac, butternut squash into a large roasting tin with the garlic. Toss with the remaining ras el hanout, remaining oil and some salt and pepper. Nestle the lamb into the tin and put in the oven to roast for 40 mins.

STEP 2

Take the lamb out of the oven and leave to rest. Put the veg back in the oven for 20 mins. Meanwhile, blitz the coriander, cumin seeds, lemon zest, lemon juice and green chilli together in a mini food processor until finely chopped and vivid green.

STEP 3

Carve the lamb, put on a platter, then pile on the veg. Sprinkle over some of the coriander mixture before taking the platter to the table for everyone to help themselves.

LITTLE SPICY VEGGIE PIES

Prep: 10 mins - Cook: 55 mins - Serves 4

INGREDIENTS

- 2 tbsp rapeseed oil
- 2 tbsp finely chopped ginger
- 3 tbsp Korma curry powder
- 3 large garlic cloves , grated
- 2 x 400g cans chickpeas , undrained
- 320g carrots , coarsely grated
- 160g frozen sweetcorn

- 1 tbsp vegetable bouillon powder
- 4 tbsp tomato purée
- 250g bag spinach , cooked

For the topping

- 750g potatoes , peeled and cut into 3cm chunks
- 1 tsp ground coriander
- 10g fresh coriander , chopped
- 150g coconut yogurt

DIRECTIONS

STEP 1

To make the topping, boil the potatoes for 15-20 mins until tender then drain, reserving the water, and mash with the ground and fresh coriander and yogurt until creamy.

STEP 2

While the potatoes are boiling, heat the oil in a large pan, add the ginger and fry briefly, tip in the curry powder and garlic, stirring quickly as you don't want it to burn, then tip in a can of chickpeas with the water from the can. Stir well, then mash in the pan to smash them up a bit, then tip in the second can of chickpeas, again with the water from the can, along with the carrots, corn, bouillon and tomato purée. Simmer for 5-10 mins, adding some of the potato water, if needed, to loosen.

STEP 3

Heat the oven to 200C/180C fan/gas 6. Spoon the filling into four individual pie dishes (each about 10cm wide, 8cm deep) and top with the mash, smoothing it to seal round the edges of the dishes. If you're following our Healthy Diet Plan, bake two for 25 mins until golden, and cook half the spinach, saving the rest of the bag for another day. Cover and chill the remaining two pies to eat another day. Will keep in the fridge for four days. If freezing, to reheat, bake from frozen for 40-45 mins until golden and piping hot.

CASHEW CURRY

Prep: 20 mins - Cook: 1 hr - Serves 3

INGREDIENTS

- 1 small onion , chopped
- 3-4 garlic cloves
- thumb-sized piece ginger , peeled and roughly chopped
- 3 green chillies , deseeded
- small pack coriander , leaves picked and stalk roughly chopped

- 100g unsalted cashews
- 2 tbsp coconut oil
- 1 ½ tbsp garam masala
- 400g can chopped tomatoes
- 450ml chicken stock
- 3 large chicken breasts (about 475g), any visible fat removed, chopped into chunks
- 155g fat-free Greek yogurt
- 10ml single cream (optional)

To serve

- 165g boiled or steamed greens (choose from spinach, kale, runner beans, asparagus or broccoli)

DIRECTIONS

STEP 1

Put the onion, garlic, ginger, chillies and coriander stalks in a small food processor and blitz to a paste.

STEP 2

Heat a large, non-stick frying pan over a medium heat. Add the cashews and toast for 1-2 mins until light golden. Set aside and return the pan to the heat. Add the oil and stir-fry the paste for 5 mins to soften. Add the garam masala and cook for a further 2 mins.

STEP 3

Add the tomatoes and stock to the pan. Mix well, then tip into a blender with the cashews and blitz until smooth. Return to the pan, season and bring to the boil, then lower to a simmer.

STEP 4

Cook for 30 mins until the sauce has thickened then add the chicken, cover with a lid and simmer for another 15 mins, until the chicken is cooked through. Add the yogurt and cream (if using), and stir well to make a creamy sauce.

STEP 5

Scatter with the coriander leaves and serve with the greens.

HARISSA-CRUMBED FISH WITH LENTILS & PEPPERS

Prep: 15 mins - Cook: 15 mins - Serves 4

INGREDIENTS

- 2 x 200g pouches cooked puy lentils
- 200g jar roasted red peppers , drained and torn into chunks
- 50g black olives , from a jar, roughly chopped
- 1 lemon , zested and cut into wedges
- 3 tbsp olive or rapeseed oil
- 4 x 140g cod fillets (or another white fish)
- 100g fresh breadcrumbs
- 1 tbsp harissa
- ½ small pack flat-leaf parsley , chopped

DIRECTIONS

STEP 1

Heat oven to 200C/180C fan/gas 6. Mix the lentils, peppers, olives, lemon zest, 2 tbsp oil and some seasoning in a roasting tin. Top with the fish fillets. Mix the breadcrumbs, harissa and the remaining oil and put a few spoonfuls on top of each piece of fish. Bake for 12-15 mins until the fish is cooked, the topping is crispy and the lentils are hot. Scatter with the parsley and squeeze over the lemon wedges.

GINGER, SESAME AND CHILLI PRAWN & BROCCOLI STIR-FRY

Prep: 5 mins - Cook: 10 mins - Serves 2

INGREDIENTS

- 250g broccoli , thin-stemmed if you like, cut into even-sized florets
- 2 balls stem ginger , finely chopped, plus 2 tbsp syrup from the jar
- 3 tbsp low-salt soy sauce
- 1 garlic clove , crushed
- 1 red chilli , a little thinly sliced, the rest deseeded and finely chopped
- 2 tsp sesame seeds
- ½ tbsp sesame oil
- 200g raw king prawns
- 100g beansprouts
- cooked rice or noodles, to serve

DIRECTIONS

STEP 1

Heat a pan of water until boiling. Tip in the broccoli and cook for just 1 min – it should still have a good crunch. Meanwhile, mix the stem ginger and syrup, soy sauce, garlic and finely chopped chilli.

STEP 2

Toast the sesame seeds in a dry wok or large frying pan. When they're nicely browned, turn up the heat and add the oil, prawns and cooked broccoli. Stir-fry for a few mins until the prawns turn pink. Pour over the ginger sauce, then tip in the beansprouts. Cook for 30 seconds, or until the beansprouts are heated thoroughly, adding a splash more soy or ginger syrup, if you like. Scatter with the sliced chilli and serve over rice or noodles.

TURKEY MEATLOAF

Prep: 15 mins - Cook: 55 mins - Serves 4

INGREDIENTS

- 1 tbsp olive oil
- 1 large onion , finely chopped
- 1 garlic clove , crushed
- 2 tbsp Worcestershire sauce
- 2 tsp tomato purée , plus 1 tbsp for the beans
- 500g turkey mince (thigh is best)
- 1 large egg , beaten
- 85g fresh white breadcrumbs
- 2 tbsp barbecue sauce , plus 4 tbsp for the beans
- 2 x 400g cans cannellini beans
- 1-2 tbsp roughly chopped parsley

DIRECTIONS

STEP 1

Heat oven to 180C/160C fan/gas 4. Heat the oil in a large frying pan and cook the onion for 8-10 mins until softened. Add the garlic, Worcestershire sauce and 2 tsp tomato purée, and stir until combined. Set aside to cool.

STEP 2

Put the turkey mince, egg, breadcrumbs and cooled onion mix in a large bowl and season well. Mix everything to combine, then shape into a rectangular loaf and place in a large roasting tin. Spread 2 tbsp barbecue sauce over the meatloaf and bake for 30 mins.

STEP 3

Meanwhile, drain 1 can of beans only, then pour both cans into a large bowl. Add the remaining barbecue sauce and tomato purée. Season and set aside.

STEP 4

When the meatloaf has had its initial cooking time, scatter the beans around the outside and bake for 15 mins more until the meatloaf is cooked through and the beans are piping hot. Scatter over the parsley and serve the meatloaf in slices.

PANEER JALFREZI WITH CUMIN RICE

Prep: 20 mins - Cook: 30 mins - Serves 4

INGREDIENTS

- 2 tsp cold-pressed rapeseed oil
- 1 large and 1 medium onion , large one finely chopped and medium one cut into wedges
- 2 large garlic cloves , chopped
- 50g ginger , peeled and shredded
- 2 tsp ground coriander
- 2 tsp cumin seeds
- 400g can chopped tomatoes
- 1 tbsp vegetable bouillon powder
- 135g paneer , chopped
- 2 large peppers , seeded and chopped
- 1 red or green chilli , deseeded and sliced
- 25g coriander , chopped

For the rice

- 260g brown basmati rice
- 1 tsp cumin seeds

DIRECTIONS

STEP 1

Heat 1 tsp oil a large non-stick frying pan and fry the chopped onions, garlic and half the ginger for 5 mins until softened. Add the ground coriander and cumin seeds and cook for 1 min more, then tip in the tomatoes, half a can of water and the bouillon. Blitz everything together with a stick blender until very smooth, then bring to a simmer. Cover and cook for 15 mins.

STEP 2

Meanwhile, cook the rice and cumin seeds in a pan of boiling water for 25 mins, or until tender.

STEP 3

Heat the remaining oil in a non-stick wok and fry the paneer until lightly coloured. Remove from the pan and set aside. Add the peppers, onion wedges and chilli to the pan and stir-fry until the veg is tender, but still retains some bite. Mix the stir-fried veg and paneer into the sauce with the chopped coriander, then serve with the rice. If you're following our Healthy Diet Plan, eat two portions of the curry and rice, then chill the rest for another day. Will keep for up to three days, covered, in the fridge. To serve on the second night, reheat the leftover portions in the microwave until piping hot.

LOW 'N' SLOW RIB STEAK WITH CUBAN MOJO SALSA

Prep: 20 mins - Cook: 3 hrs and 20 mins - Serves 2

INGREDIENTS

- 1 rib steak on the bone or côte du boeuf (about 800g)
- 1 tbsp rapeseed oil
- 1 garlic clove
- 2 thyme sprigs
- 25g butter , chopped into small pieces
- sweet potato fries
- a dressed salad , to serve

For the mojo salsa

- 2 limes
- 1 small orange
- ½ small bunch mint , finely chopped
- small bunch coriander , finely chopped
- 4 spring onions , finely chopped
- 1 small garlic clove , crushed
- 1 fat green chilli , finely chopped
- 4 tbsp extra virgin rapeseed oil or olive oil

DIRECTIONS

STEP 1

Leave the beef at room temperature for about 1 hr before you cook it. Heat oven to 60C/40C fan/gas 1 /4 if you like your beef medium rare, or 65C/45C fan/gas 1 /4 for medium. (Cooking at these low temperatures will be more accurate in an electric oven than in a gas one. If using gas, put the oven on the lowest setting you have, and be aware that the cooking time may be shorter.)

STEP 2

Put the unseasoned beef in a heavy-based ovenproof frying pan. Cook in the middle of the oven for 3 hrs undisturbed.

STEP 3

Meanwhile, make the salsa. Zest the limes and orange into a bowl. Cut each in half and place, cut-side down, in a hot pan. Cook for a few mins until the fruits are charred, then squeeze the juice into the bowl. Add the other ingredients and season well.

STEP 4

When the beef is cooked, it should look dry on the surface, and dark pink in colour. If you have a meat thermometer, test the internal temperature – it should be 58-60C. Remove the pan from the oven and set over a high heat on the hob. Add the oil and sear the meat on both sides for a few mins until caramelised. Sear the fat for a few mins too. Smash the garlic clove with the heel of your hand and add this to the pan with the thyme and butter. When the butter is foaming, spoon it over the beef and cook for another 1-2 mins. Transfer the beef to a warm plate, cover with foil, and leave to rest for 5-10 mins. Carve away from the bone and into slices before serving with the salsa, fries and salad.

ASPARAGUS & BROAD BEAN LASAGNE

Prep: 35 mins - Cook: 1 hr and 10 mins - Serves 4

INGREDIENTS

- 225ml whole milk
- 320g frozen baby broad beans
- 3 garlic cloves , chopped
- 30g pack fresh basil , roughly chopped
- ½ lemon , zested
- 4 spring onions , chopped
- 1 tsp vegetable bouillon powder
- 6 wholemeal lasagne sheets
- 320g frozen peas
- 2 x 300g tubs low-fat cottage cheese
- 1 egg
- whole nutmeg , for grating
- 250g asparagus , woody ends trimmed
- 25g parmesan or vegetarian alternative, finely grated

DIRECTIONS

STEP 1

Heat oven to 180C/160C fan/gas 4. Heat the milk in a pan until just boiling, then tip in the beans (add a splash of water to cover if you need to). Cook for 3 mins to defrost, then add the garlic, basil, lemon zest, spring onions and bouillon, then blitz for a few mins with a hand blender until smooth.

STEP 2

Spoon half the purée into a 20 x 26cm ovenproof dish. Top with 3 lasagne sheets, the remaining purée, and the peas, then the remaining lasagne sheets.

STEP 3

Whisk the cottage cheese with the egg and a good grating of nutmeg. Pour over the lasagne, then press in the asparagus and scatter over the parmesan. Bake for 1 hr until golden and a knife easily slides through. Can be kept chilled for two days.

SMOKY CHICKPEAS ON TOAST

Prep: 2 mins - Cook: 10 mins - Serves 2

INGREDIENTS

- 1 tsp olive oil or vegetable oil, plus a drizzle
- 1 small onion or banana shallot, chopped
- 2 tsp chipotle paste
- 250ml passata
- 400g can chickpeas , drained
- 2 tsp honey
- 2 tsp red wine vinegar
- 2-4 slices good crusty bread
- 2 eggs

DIRECTIONS

STEP 1

Heat ½ tsp of the oil in a pan. Tip in the onion and cook until soft, about 5-8 mins, then add the chipotle paste, passata, chickpeas, honey and vinegar. Season and bubble for 5 mins.

STEP 2

Toast the bread. Heat the remaining oil in a frying pan and fry the eggs. Drizzle the toast with a little oil, then top with the chickpeas and fried eggs.

FENNEL SPAGHETTI

Prep: 15 mins - Cook: 30 mins - Serves 2

INGREDIENTS

- 1 tbsp olive oil , plus extra for serving
- 1 tsp fennel seeds
- 2 small garlic cloves , 1 crushed, 1 thinly sliced
- 1 lemon , zested and juiced
- 1 fennel bulb , finely sliced, fronds reserved
- 150g spaghetti
- ½ pack flat-leaf parsley , chopped
- shaved parmesan (or vegetarian alternative), to serve (optional)

DIRECTIONS

STEP 1

Heat the oil in a frying pan over a medium heat and cook the fennel seeds until they pop. Sizzle the garlic for 1 min, then add the lemon zest and half the fennel slices. Cook for 10-12 mins or until the fennel has softened.

STEP 2

Meanwhile, bring a pan of salted water to the boil and cook the pasta for 1 min less than pack instructions. Use tongs to transfer the pasta to the frying pan along with a good splash of pasta water. Increase the heat to high and toss well. Stir through the remaining fennel slices, the parsley and lemon juice, season generously, then tip straight into two bowls to serve. Top with the fennel fronds, extra olive oil and parmesan shavings, if you like.

HEALTHY BOLOGNESE

Prep: 5 mins - Cook: 20 mins - 2 generously, 4 as a snack

INGREDIENTS

- 100g wholewheat linguine
- 2 tsp rapeseed oil
- 1 fennel bulb , finely chopped
- 2 garlic cloves , sliced
- 200g pork mince with less than 5% fat
- 200g whole cherry tomatoes

- 1 tbsp balsamic vinegar
- 1 tsp vegetable bouillon powder
- generous handful chopped basil

DIRECTIONS

STEP 1

Bring a large pan of water to the boil, then cook the linguine following pack instructions, about 10 mins.

STEP 2

Meanwhile, heat the oil in a non-stick wok or wide pan. Add the fennel and garlic and cook, stirring every now and then, until tender, about 10 mins.

STEP 3

Tip in the pork and stir-fry until it changes colour, breaking it up as you go so there are no large clumps. Add the tomatoes, vinegar and bouillon, then cover the pan and cook for 10 mins over a low heat until the tomatoes burst and the pork is cooked and tender. Add the linguine and basil and plenty of pepper, and toss well before serving.

VIETNAMESE CHICKEN NOODLE SOUP

Prep: 20 mins - Cook: 25 mins - Serves 6

INGREDIENTS

- 1 tbsp vegetable oil
- 3 shallots, sliced
- 3 garlic cloves, sliced
- 1 lemongrass stalk, chopped
- 2.5cm piece ginger, sliced
- 3 star anise
- 1 cinnamon stick
- 1 tsp coriander seeds
- ¼ tsp Chinese five spice
- ¼ tsp black peppercorns
- 1 tsp caster sugar
- 1 tbsp fish sauce
- 1.25 - 1.5 litres good quality fresh chicken stock
- 3 large chicken breasts (about 500g)

To serve

- 450g rice noodles
- 4 spring onions, finely sliced on an angle
- 1 carrot, shredded or peeled into ribbon with a vegetable peeler
- 2 large handfuls (150g) mung bean sprouts
- large bunch coriander, chopped
- small bunch mint, leaves chopped
- 1 red chilli, thinly sliced (optional)
- 2 tbsp crispy fried shallots (optional)
- 1 kaffir lime leaf, tough central stalk removed, very finely sliced, (optional)
- 1 lime, cut into wedges

DIRECTIONS

STEP 1

Heat the oil in a small frying pan on medium heat and gently cook the shallots and garlic until caramelised and golden brown (about 4-5 mins).

STEP 2

In a large saucepan, add the caramelised shallots and garlic, lemongrass, ginger, star anise, cinnamon stick, coriander seeds, Chinese five-spice, peppercorns, sugar, fish sauce, chicken stock and chicken breasts. Cover with a lid and bring to a very gentle simmer for about 15 mins.

STEP 3

Meanwhile, cook the noodles, following pack instructions, until just cooked through (do not over-cook). Rinse under cold water to prevent them sticking together. Drain and divide between serving bowls.

STEP 4

Strain the soup through a sieve. Discard the spices. Shred the chicken and keep to one side. Return soup to the pot and bring to a boil. Season to taste with more fish sauce if needed.

STEP 5

To serve, ladle piping hot soup into bowls of noodles and chicken, and top with spring onion, carrot, bean sprouts, and herbs, plus the chilli, crispy shallots and kaffir lime leaf if using. Serve with a lime wedge to squeeze over, and more fish sauce and chilli to taste.

ROAST ROOTS WITH GOAT'S CHEESE & SPINACH

INGREDIENTS

- 350g butternut squash , deseeded and cut into chunks, peeled if you like
- 200g carrots , peeled and cut into long batons
- 250g parsnips , peeled and cut into long batons
- 200g raw beetroot , well-scrubbed and cut into thick wedges
- 1 medium red onion , cut into wedges
- 1 tbsp cold-pressed rapeseed oil
- juice and finely grated zest 1 lemon
- 1 bulb garlic , cloves separated
- 4-5 thyme sprigs , leaves roughly chopped
- 75g soft rindless goat's cheese log
- 25g mixed nuts , such as brazils, almonds, hazelnuts, pecans and walnuts, roughly chopped
- 50g baby leaf spinach

DIRECTIONS

STEP 1

Heat oven to 200C/180C fan/gas 6. Put the vegetables, without the garlic, into a bowl and toss with the oil, lemon zest and juice and plenty of ground black pepper.

STEP 2

Scatter the vegetables over a large baking tray or roasting tin and bake for 30 mins. Take the tray out of the oven, add the garlic and thyme, then turn the vegetables. Return to the oven for 20 mins or until the vegetables are tender and lightly browned, turning halfway through. Dot with the goat's cheese and nuts, scatter over the spinach and return to the oven for 3-5 mins or until the spinach has wilted and the goat's cheese has begun to melt. You can press the softened garlic cloves out of their skins and mash with the roasted vegetables, if you like.

SPICE-CRUSTED AUBERGINES & PEPPERS WITH PILAF

Prep: 10 mins - Cook: 30 mins - Serves 4

INGREDIENTS

- 2 large aubergines , halved

- 2 tbsp extra virgin olive oil
- 2 red peppers , quartered
- 2 tsp ground cinnamon
- 2 tsp chilli flakes
- 2 tsp za'atar
- 4 tbsp pomegranate molasses
- 140g puy lentils
- 140g basmati rice
- seeds from 1 pomegranate
- small pack flat-leaf parsley , roughly chopped
- Greek or coconut yogurt , to serve

DIRECTIONS

STEP 1

Heat oven to 220C/200C fan/gas 7. Using a sharp knife, score a diamond pattern into the aubergines. Brush with 1 tbsp of the oil, season well and place on a baking tray, cut-side down. Cook in the oven for 15 mins. Add the peppers to the tray, turn the aubergines over and drizzle everything with the remaining oil. Sprinkle over the spices, 1 tbsp of the pomegranate molasses and a little salt. Roast in the oven for 15 mins more.

STEP 2

Boil the lentils in plenty of water until al dente. After they've been boiling for 5 mins, add the rice. Cook for 10 mins or until cooked through but with a bit of bite. Drain and return to the pan, covered with a lid to keep warm.

STEP 3

Stir the pomegranate seeds and parsley through the lentil rice. Divide between four plates or tip onto a large platter. Top with the roasted veg, a dollop of yogurt and the remaining pomegranate molasses drizzled over.

POTATO PANCAKES WITH CHARD & EGGS

Prep: 10 mins - Cook: 15 mins - Serves 2

INGREDIENTS

- 300g mashed potato
- 4 spring onions , very finely chopped
- 25g plain wholemeal flour
- ½ tsp baking powder

- 3 eggs
- 2 tsp rapeseed oil
- 240g chard , stalks and leaves roughly chopped, or baby spinach, chopped

DIRECTIONS

STEP 1

Mix the mash, spring onions, flour, baking powder and 1 of the eggs in a bowl. Heat the oil in a non-stick frying pan, then spoon in the potato mix to make two mounds. Flatten them to form two 15cm discs and fry for 5-8 mins until the undersides are set and golden, then carefully ip over and cook on the other side.

STEP 2

Meanwhile, wash the chard and put in a pan with some of the water still clinging to it, then cover and cook over a medium heat for 5 mins until wilted and tender. Poach the remaining eggs.

STEP 3

Top the pancakes with the greens and egg. Serve while the yolks are still runny.

ROASTED TOMATO, BASIL & PARMESAN QUICHE

Prep: 40 mins - Cook: 40 mins - Serves 8

INGREDIENTS

- 300g cherry tomato
- drizzle olive oil
- 50g parmesan (or vegetarian alternative), grated
- 2 eggs
- 284ml pot double cream
- handful basil leaves, shredded, plus a few small ones left whole for scattering

For the pastry

- 280g plain flour, plus extra for dusting
- 140g cold butter, cut into pieces

DIRECTIONS

STEP 1

To make the pastry, tip the flour and butter into a bowl, then rub together with your fingertips until completely mixed and crumbly. Add 8 tbsp cold water, then bring everything together with your hands until just combined. Roll into a ball and use straight away or chill for up to 2 days. The pastry can also be frozen for up to a month.

STEP 2

Roll out the pastry on a lightly floured surface to a round about 5cm larger than a 25cm tin. Use your rolling pin to lift it up, then drape over the tart case so there is an overhang of pastry on the sides. Using a small ball of pastry scraps, push the pastry into the corners of the tin. Chill in the fridge or freezer for 20 mins. Heat oven to 200C/fan 180C/gas 6.

STEP 3

In a small roasting tin, drizzle the tomatoes with olive oil and season with salt and pepper. Put the tomatoes in a low shelf of the oven.

STEP 4

Lightly prick the base of the tart with a fork, line the tart case with a large circle of greaseproof paper or foil, then fill with baking beans. Blind-bake the tart for 20 mins, remove the paper and beans, then continue to cook for 5-10 mins until biscuit brown.

STEP 5

When you remove the tart case from the oven, take out the tomatoes, too.

STEP 6

While the tart is cooking, beat the eggs in a large bowl. Gradually add the cream, then stir in the basil and season. When the case is ready, sprinkle half the cheese over the base, scatter over the tomatoes, pour over the cream mix, then finally scatter over the rest of the cheese. Bake for 20-25 mins until set and golden brown. Leave to cool in the case, trim the edges of the pastry, then remove from the tin. Scatter over the remaining basil and serve in slices.

ROSEMARY CHICKEN WITH TOMATO SAUCE

Prep: 5 mins - Cook: 30 mins - Serves 4

INGREDIENTS

* 1 tbsp olive oil

- 8 boneless, skinless chicken thighs
- 1 rosemary sprig, leaves finely chopped
- 1 red onion, finely sliced
- 3 garlic cloves, sliced
- 2 anchovy fillets, chopped
- 400g can chopped tomatoes
- 1 tbsp capers, drained
- 75ml red wine (optional)

DIRECTIONS

STEP 1

Heat half the oil in a non-stick pan, then brown the chicken all over. Add half the chopped rosemary, stir to coat, then set aside on a plate.

STEP 2

In the same pan, heat the rest of the oil, then gently cook the onion for about 5 mins until soft. Add the garlic, anchovies and remaining rosemary, then fry for a few mins more until fragrant. Pour in the tomatoes and capers with the wine, if using, or 75ml water if not. Bring to the boil, then return the chicken pieces to the pan. Cover, then cook for 20 mins until the chicken is cooked through. Season and serve with a crisp green salad and crusty bread.

PENNE WITH CHORIZO & BROCCOLI

Prep: 5 mins - Cook: 20 mins - Serves 4

INGREDIENTS

- 400g penne
- small head of broccoli , broken into small florets
- 200g cooking chorizo , diced
- 2 garlic cloves , crushed
- 1 tbsp fennel seed
- 200g low-fat cream cheese with garlic & herbs
- parmesan and rocket leaves, to serve

DIRECTIONS

STEP 1

Cook the penne following pack instructions, adding the broccoli for the final 3 mins. When cooked, drain, reserving a splash of the cooking water.

STEP 2

Meanwhile, fry the chorizo in a large dry frying pan until it starts to turn golden and release its oils. Add the garlic and fennel seeds, and cook for 1 min more. When the penne is cooked, tip it into the pan with the chorizo. Add the cream cheese, stir together until melted, adding a splash of the reserved cooking water so the sauce coats the pasta.

STEP 3

Serve in bowls, scattered with a few rocket leaves and some grated Parmesan, if you like.

BROCCOLI PASTA SHELLS

Prep: 5 mins - Cook: 15 mins - Serves 4

INGREDIENTS

- 1 head of broccoli, chopped into florets
- 1 garlic clove, unpeeled
- 2 tbsp olive oil
- 250g pasta shells
- ½ small pack parsley
- ½ small pack basil
- 30g toasted pine nuts
- ½ lemon, zested and juiced
- 30g parmesan (or vegetarian alternative), plus extra to serve

DIRECTIONS

STEP 1

Heat the oven to 200C/180C fan/gas 6. Toss the broccoli and garlic in 1 tbsp of the olive oil on a roasting tray and roast in the oven for 10-12 mins, until softened.

STEP 2

Tip the pasta shells into a pan of boiling, salted water. Cook according to packet instructions and drain. Tip the parsley, basil, pine nuts, lemon juice and parmesan into a blender. Once the broccoli is done, set aside a few of the smaller pieces. Squeeze the garlic from its skin, add to the blender along with the rest of the broccoli, pulse to a pesto and season well.

STEP 3

Toss the pasta with the pesto. Add the reserved broccoli florets, split between two bowls and top with a little extra parmesan, the lemon zest and a good grinding of black pepper, if you like.

GINGER CHICKEN & GREEN BEAN NOODLES

Prep: 10 mins - Cook: 15 mins - Serves 2

INGREDIENTS

- ½ tbsp vegetable oil
- 2 skinless chicken breasts, sliced
- 200g green beans , trimmed and halved crosswise
- thumb-sized piece of ginger , peeled and cut into matchsticks
- 2 garlic cloves , sliced
- 1 ball stem ginger , finely sliced, plus 1 tsp syrup from the jar
- 1 tsp cornflour , mixed with 1 tbsp water
- 1 tsp dark soy sauce , plus extra to serve (optional)
- 2 tsp rice vinegar
- 200g cooked egg noodles

DIRECTIONS

STEP 1

Heat the oil in a wok over a high heat and stir-fry the chicken for 5 mins. Add the green beans and stir-fry for 4-5 mins more until the green beans are just tender, and the chicken is just cooked through.

STEP 2

Stir in the fresh ginger and garlic, and stir-fry for 2 mins, then add the stem ginger and syrup, the cornflour mix, soy sauce and vinegar. Stir-fry for 1 min, then toss in the noodles. Cook until everything is hot and the sauce coats the noodles. Drizzle with more soy, if you like, and serve.

POTATO, PEA & EGG CURRY ROTIS

Prep: 5 mins - Cook: 25 mins - Serves 4

INGREDIENTS

- 1 tbsp oil
- 2 tbsp mild curry paste
- 400g can chopped tomatoes

* 2 potatoes , cut into small chunks
* 200g peas
* 3 eggs , hard-boiled
* pack rotis , warmed through
* 150g tub natural yogurt , to serve

DIRECTIONS

STEP 1

Heat the oil in a saucepan and briefly fry the curry paste. Tip in the tomatoes and half a can of water and bring to a simmer. Add the potatoes and cook for 20 mins, or until the potato is tender. Stir in the peas and cook for 3 mins.

STEP 2

Halve the eggs and place them on top of the curry, then warm everything through. Serve with the rotis and yogurt on the side.

SOUP MAKER TOMATO SOUP

Prep: 5 mins - Cook: 30 mins - Serves 2

INGREDIENTS

* 500g ripe tomatoes , off the vine and quartered or halved
* 1 small onion , chopped
* ½ small carrot , chopped
* ½ celery stick, chopped
* 1 tsp tomato purée
* pinch of sugar
* 450ml vegetable stock

DIRECTIONS

STEP 1

Put all the ingredients into the soup maker and press the 'smooth soup' function. Make sure you don't fill the soup maker above the max fill line.

STEP 2

Once the cycle is complete, season well, and check the soup for sweetness. Add a little more sugar, salt or tomato puree for depth of colour, if you like.

LEEK, TOMATO & BARLEY RISOTTO WITH PAN-COOKED COD

Prep: 10 mins - Cook: 20 mins - Serves 2

INGREDIENTS

- 2 tsp rapeseed oil
- 1 large leek (315g), thinly sliced
- 2 garlic cloves , chopped
- 400g can barley (don't drain)
- 2 tsp vegetable bouillon
- 1 tsp finely chopped sage
- 1 tbsp thyme leaves , plus a few extra to serve
- 160g cherry tomatoes
- 50g finely grated parmesan
- 2 skin-on cod fillets or firm white fish fillets

DIRECTIONS

STEP 1

Heat 1 tsp oil in a non-stick pan and fry the leek and garlic for 5-10 mins, stirring frequently until softened, adding a splash of water to help it cook if you need to.

STEP 2

Tip in the barley with its liquid, then stir in the bouillon, sage and thyme. Simmer, stirring frequently for 3-4 mins. Add the tomatoes and cook about 4-5 mins more until they soften and start to split, adding a drop more water if necessary. Stir in the parmesan.

STEP 3

Meanwhile, heat the remaining oil in a non-stick pan and fry the cod, skin-side down, for 4-5 mins. Flip the fillets over to cook briefly on the other side. Spoon the risotto into two bowls. Serve the cod on top with a few thyme leaves, if you like.